The Franco-Calgarians

French Language, Leisure, and Linguistic Life-style in an Anglophone City

Many of North America's francophones live and work in large anglophone cities, immersed in overwhelmingly English-speaking environments, yet they manage to keep their language and culture alive. In this study Robert A. Stebbins finds that francophone culture in Calgary flourishes primarily through leisure activities.

Stebbins was a participant and an observer in Calgary's French community between 1987 and 1992. In 1992 he conducted unstructured interviews in French with eighty-five adult respondents, focusing on their patterns of everyday personal and collective life. His book reveals that in large cities such as Calgary, francophone populations form communities through social and cultural organization rather than geographical association. In these circumstances, family, household, school, and leisure activities are key to maintaining French language and culture and promoting individual and community development.

This is the first ethnographic study of the francophone community of a major anglophone urban centre in Canada. Stebbins presents an objective but sympathetic analysis in a fluid and engaging style. His work provides a prototype for the analysis of francophone communities in anglophone cities.

ROBERT A. STEBBINS is Professor, Department of Sociology, University of Calgary.

The Franco-Calgarians

French Language, Leisure, and Linguistic Life-style in an Anglophone City

ROBERT A. STEBBINS

UNIVERSITY OF TORONTO PRESS
Toronto Buffalo London

© University of Toronto Press Incorporated 1994
Toronto Buffalo London
Printed in Canada

ISBN 0-8020-0611-6 (cloth)
ISBN 0-8020-7577-0 (paper)

Printed on acid-free paper

Canadian Cataloguing in Publication Data

Stebbins, Robert A., 1938–
    The Franco-Calgarians : French language, leisure,
    and linguistic life-style in an anglophone city

    Includes bibliographical references and index.
    ISBN 0-8020-0611-6 (bound) ISBN 0-8020-7577-0 (pbk.)

    1. Canadians, French-speaking – Alberta – Calgary.*
    2. French language – Alberta – Calgary.
    3. Minorities – Alberta – Calgary. I. Title.

    FC3697.9.F74S74 1994   305.811'40712338
    F1099.5.C35S74 1994   C94-931190-1

This book has been published with the help of a grant from the Social
Science Federation of Canada, using funds provided by the Social Sciences
and Humanities Research Council of Canada.

À Donna et Henri Mydlarski

Contents

Preface

One could say that this book serves as proof of my determination to learn French in a city where the language is rarely heard in public, where francophones make up barely 2 per cent of the population, and where anglophones who constitute the majority view such people as just another ethnic group. During my school days I acquired a reading knowledge of two other European languages while carefully avoiding la belle langue, which was rumoured to be difficult. As my professional career unfolded this linguistic deficiency became increasingly burdensome, in no small part due to the sense of interpersonal unfairness it engendered when my French-Canadian colleagues would struggle with English while I could do nothing to ease their discomfort by speaking with them in French. By early 1984 this injustice troubled me to the point where I decided I must assuage it – an expensive decision it turned out, for 120 lessons at Berlitz are not exactly bon marché.

The lessons I received at Berlitz and the subsequent language courses I took at the Alliance Française and the French Centre at the University of Calgary were well done, but for all that still insufficient. Although I clearly needed more immersion in the language than the classroom could provide, the chances of finding it in Calgary seemed remote. It was around this time that I came across the Association Canadienne-Française de l'Alberta, the main organizational mouthpiece for Franco-Albertans. I decided to join. As part of my membership I began receiving its weekly newspaper, *Le*

Franco, an organ that opened up a fascinating new social world of which I was almost totally ignorant, notwithstanding my considerable knowledge about Calgary in general. In *Le Franco* I read about the different French-language clubs, events, activities, and organizations in the city, about its French school, École Sainte-Anne, and about its French parish, Église Sainte-Famille. I also read about the prominent families and individuals whose influence has shaped the local French community since the late nineteenth century. From all this I learned that Franco-Calgarians are immensely proud of their language and culture and fiercely determined to maintain this heritage, transmit it to their children, and develop still further as a distinct linguistic collectivity.

As my proficiency in French grew I joined more groups and participated in more activities, spurred on now as much by sociological curiosity as by the need to leave the artificial world of the classroom for the real world of routine francophone affairs. With this deepening involvement came the realization that Franco-Calgarians are maintaining their language and even advancing their community against the heavy odds of the powerful influence of the surrounding anglophone culture. What they have done is to treat the processes of maintenance, transmission, and development of French culture as goals to be pursued in everyday life, as goals to be incorporated into their linguistic life-styles. By this time I had read enough of the sociological literature on Canadian French communities outside Quebec to learn that this rosy view of their social and cultural survival was not widely shared by my colleagues. I also learned that the linguistic life-styles of francophones living in Canada's large anglophone cities had never been explored.

It soon became evident that the processes of French linguistic and cultural maintenance, transmission, and development are at the very centre of the struggle for survival of French Canada outside Quebec. There was no turning back now; the sociologist in me yearned to know more about these processes and the people who give them concrete expression. By this time I was sufficiently fluent in French to use it in my fieldwork, for I had interviewed in that language during an earlier study of stand-up comics. True, I was hardly an accomplished speaker, but I could communicate and could always improve.

I had completed several years of observation when I joined Yvonne Hébert, a Franco-Albertan and professor of education at the University of Calgary, in a preliminary demographic survey of Calgary francophones and francophiles. We needed as background for our separate research projects a social profile of the city's French-speaking population. For me, the profile served as a stan-dard against which I could measure the representativeness of the sample I had selected for interviewing in the present study, an exploratory-qualitative investigation of French language, leisure, and linguistic life-style.

As the possibility of doing fieldwork in French on Calgary's francophones became ever more likely, I saw myself abandoning active research in serious leisure, a domain that had occupied me intensely since the early 1970s. But, alas, I had become sensitized to the essential features of leisure, which I now began to see every-where in the linguistic life-styles I was observing. I soon realized that in a city such as Calgary, leisure is as vital to the maintenance, transmission, and development of French language, culture, and community as the family and the French school are. Indeed, it appears that leisure has largely replaced work as one of the core institutions in urban French communities lying outside Quebec. I believe this study demonstrates that without a substantially devel-oped leisure sector, these communities would soon suffer death by assimilation to the anglophone world in which they are embedded.

A small number of people have faithfully served as mentors throughout all this. They are Alain Bertrand, Léo Boileau, Jeanne and Jean-Pierre Deslauriers, Yvonne Hébert, Donna and Henri Mydlarski, and Antoine Sassine. Sometimes they advised me on aspects of the Calgary French community and related matters, sometimes they helped me over the linguistic hurdles inevitably encountered by anyone who tries to learn another language. I doubt this study could have been undertaken without their contin-ual support. Nor could it have been undertaken without the keen desire to know themselves shown by the many Franco-Calgarians with whom I have come contact, especially those who consented to be interviewed. Their interest in this study was, and still is, extremely high, giving substance to my conviction that few aspects of life are as pervasive and deeply rooted as a person's language and its related culture. I am also deeply grateful to Barbara Christian who meticulously copy-edited the manuscript, thereby adding significantly to its accuracy and readability.

The data collection was funded from two sources. The Multicultural Directorate of the Secretary of State provided funding for the demographic phase. The fieldwork phase was supported by the Social Science and Humanities Research Council of Canada with funds administered through the Research Grants Committee at the University of Calgary.

The Franco-Calgarians

French Language, Leisure, and Linguistic Life-style in an Anglophone City

1

Francophones in the City

The French and English word *francophone*, which is generally spelled and defined the same the world over, is nonetheless sometimes used in Canada in a special way that requires clarification at the outset. According to Canadian usage a francophone is someone who learned French as his or her first language, a person for whom it is not only a mother tongue but also a tongue that he or she can still understand.[1] *Anglophones* are those whose mother tongue is English. In Canada the term *francophile* is used by some speakers to describe people who routinely speak (and, more rarely, write) French as a second language.

Dictionaries, whether French or English, whether published in Canada or elsewhere, do not acknowledge these Canadian definitions; the dictionary definitions of these terms are substantially different. The *Petit Robert*, for example, defines as a francophile someone who likes France and the French. Be that as it may, my observations suggest that the special Canadian usage of francophone, anglophone, and francophile was pioneered by social scientists to help them make sense of the complicated linguistic environment in which Canadians have lived since Quebec's Quiet Revolution in the 1960s. Today this usage has gained a degree of currency among the lay public in Canada, although more so, it appears, among francophones than anglophones. Since this is a study of Canadians, their usage of the three terms is the one we will adopt in this book.

In Canada and other parts of the world where French-speaking people form a linguistic minority, local francophones and a smaller number of francophiles coalesce into community-like structures known in French as *francophonies*. This term, which is also part of the conceptual backbone of this book, has a number of advantages over its cousin, *community*. As a scientific term the latter remains controversial, weakened by a professional dispute over whether a geographical or territorial basis is an essential quality of a true community (Almgren 1992). There is also debate about the degree of self-sufficiency or completeness a group of people must achieve before they can be said to meet one of the many sociological definitions of community.[2] The term francophonie allows us to escape such notional wrangling while retaining the capacity to speak of an *ethnic formation* of some sort (Breton et al. 1990: 4–9), based on a moderate degree of completeness and rooted in a set of organizations and a vast network of interpersonal relationships with no clear geographical locus (Goldenberg and Haines 1992). Moreover francophonie is a folk concept, and good ethnographies, of which I hope this study will be seen as an example, incorporate numerous concepts of this nature as a way of communicating the outlook of the people observed.

Having said all this, it is evident that I use the word community in many places in this book, always as a stylistic alternative to fran-cophonie. As I have come to realize, it is an idea that sociologists can live neither with nor without. The nearest terminological equivalent in sociology to francophonie is Anthony Cohen's (1985) concept of symbolic community, the essence of which is contained in the proposition that 'the reality of community lies in its members' perception of the vitality of its culture. People construct community symbolically, making it a resource and repository of meaning, and a referent of their identity' (Cohen 1985: 118). My use of community here conforms to this conception as does the descriptor *francophonie invisible*, which is current among French-speaking Calgarians.

Outside the anglophone majority, francophones constitute by far the largest linguistic group in Canada – approximately a quarter of the population in 1991. Moreover, according to the 1991 census

(Statistics Canada 1992), 907,465 of Canada's 6,505,570 franco-phones live outside Quebec, and 257,524 or 28 per cent of the former live in the ten Census Metropolitan Areas (CMAs), areas with a population of at least 300,000 containing 8,000 or more francophones. Of these areas, Ottawa is home to the largest num-ber of francophones (estimated at 84,489), whereas the next largest concentrations are found in Toronto (49,800) and Winnipeg (29,465).[3] Calgary with its 10,535 francophones has more in com-mon with such cities as Halifax (8,690) and Hamilton (8,515). These figures describe the distribution of francophones with one mother tongue only, namely – French. All ten metropolitan areas also include additional, comparatively small, numbers of people who have two or three mother tongues, one of which is French. In Calgary in 1991, 3,955 people could be classified thus, many of whom were raised speaking French and English. This group brings the total number of francophones in that city to 14,490, or about 2 per cent of the population of the Calgary CMA.

Two important lessons can be pulled from this brief statistical portrait. One is that Canadian francophones are by no means equally distributed across the country. This suggests that life-styles should be different where francophones live in a minority situation as compared with where they live as part of the majority. The second lesson is that life-styles in mid-sized and large cities differ in many important ways from those in towns and small cities. Approximately 28 per cent of Canada's francophones who live outside Quebec now live in large cities. Their distinctive existence has prompted Réjean Beaudoin (1988: 266–9) to describe them as the *nouveaux francophones*. Sociologically speaking we know much less about them and their life-styles than about the other 72 per cent and the life-styles they lead.

The Calgary Study

The everyday involvements of francophones living in small towns and small cities have been studied from time to time, although certainly not extensively (e.g., Anderson 1985a; Gold 1975; Jackson 1988; Dawson 1936; Rayside 1991). As for research on the life-styles of big-city francophones in Canada, it is literally nonexistent. Two demographically oriented studies were carried out nearly twenty-five years ago in Toronto (Maxwell 1971) and in the enclave of Maillardville, located in exurban Vancouver (Villeneuve 1983). However, in addition to being, in many ways, outdated, the two studies centred on francophone communities demographically quite different from the one we find today in Calgary. For example, Yvonne Hébert and I discovered through our own preliminary demographic study of Calgary (Hébert and Stebbins 1993) that francophones there are largely middle- and upper-middle class and frequently employed in white-collar positions or as professionals and executives, whereas the two earlier studies described the francophonies of Toronto and Maillardville as predominantly working class. As Cardinal and Lapointe (1989) report in their review of the sociological literature on Canadian francophone communities outside Quebec, one searches in vain for studies of the inhabitants' everyday involvements in French.

Accordingly, the study reported in this book examined the everyday French language life-styles of contemporary Calgary francophones and francophiles. The observations presented here should be seen as complementing the findings emanating from the somewhat more extensive demolinguistic and social-structural research done on the French-language communities outside Quebec. Even if it has tended to ignore the events of everyday life, this research has contributed enormously to our understanding of these communities (see Anderson 1985b; Breton 1964; Association for Canadian Studies 1989). It has already been used as interpretive background in this chapter and will be further used in many places in the following pages, even if its typically pessimistic conclusions are challenged in the final two chapters. In other words the present study helps fill a gap in our knowledge created by the inherent limits of demolinguistic and social-structural research, but it in no way renders obsolete the results of this research.

Studying these everyday French-language life-styles is especially important, nevertheless for such cities as Calgary, Toronto, Hamilton, Vancouver, and Halifax. These cities never had, or in the cases of Vancouver and Calgary, have not had for many years, active, geographically identifiable francophone communities.[4] By contrast, Ottawa, Winnipeg, and Edmonton have had such formations from their inception. These formations have served as significant rallying points over the years, both in the form of geographic communities – Vanier in Ottawa, Saint-Boniface in Winnipeg, Bonnie Doon in Edmonton – and in the form of symbolic communities. In the latter capacity they have ensured a notable degree of institutional continuity throughout this century, particularly in the areas of work, leisure, family, religion, and education.

Notwithstanding their lack of a geographically identifiable francophone community, Calgary, Toronto, Hamilton, and similar cities have all known increases in the absolute numbers of francophones between the census years of 1981 and 1991, as has the nation as a whole.[5] Evidence from the present study suggests that those in Calgary are not only multiplying numerically to some degree, but even thriving culturally, possibly to an equivalent degree. Yet we shall see in chapter 2 that its geographic francophone community died approximately ninety years ago. The question, then, is how do these urban francophonies survive and, if Calgary is typical, flourish, even though they lack an extended territorial foundation?

The way to begin answering this question, given the lack of prior research, is to explore as thoroughly as possible one of the cities without a geographically identifiable francophone community. That Calgary was chosen for this purpose was a matter of convenience. Studying any community ethnographically requires a great deal of participant observation, an impossible undertaking unless one lives in that community. The participation-observation for this study began in 1987 – the year I finally achieved sufficient competence in French to participate in the public affairs of the local francophonie – and continued through 1992. Between January and May of 1992, I also conducted sixty semidirected, face-to-face interviews with thirty-five individuals and twenty-five couples on the subject of their French-language life-styles (see Appendix containing the translated version of the final interview guide used to explore these life-styles). Altogether eight-five adults were interviewed, all of whom lived in greater Calgary, seventy-three of whom were raised as francophones, ten of whom were raised as anglophones who later learned French (francophiles), and two of whom were raised as francophone-anglophone bilinguals. The interviews, which averaged two hours in length, were (with three exceptions) conducted in French. For this reason quotations from the respondents excerpted in this book, unless noted otherwise, have been translated by me directly from the recorded interviews.

Why include francophiles in this or any other investigation of an urban French community in Canada? Because the observational phase of the present study strongly suggests that they are significantly involved in the French affairs of the contemporary anglophone city. For example: a francophile was recently elected to the board of directors of the local chapter of the Association Canadienne Française de l'Alberta, one of the most influential francophone organizations in town. Two others helped found a highly successful local professional club. The role of the francophiles in the Calgary French community will be evident in many places in the coming chapters.

This sample is reasonably representative of the francophone Calgarians of European and North American extraction. Thirty-eight of the respondents were born and raised in Quebec, twelve in France, ten in Alberta, ten in Ontario, eight in countries other than France (mostly European), and seven in other Canadian provinces (chiefly Manitoba, New Brunswick, and Saskatchewan). The participants had lived in the city for an average of 12.4 years, a calculation that omitted the three francophone interviewees who were born and raised in Calgary. The vast majority had at least completed high school; their highest degrees were distributed as followings: high school (twelve), collège d'enseignement général et professionnel (CÉGEP) or technical school (sixteen), bachelor's (twenty-five), professional school (fifteen), and master's or doctoral (twelve). Three others never finished high school, whereas two held specialized certificates. Those sampled worked in a wide range of occupations, although they tended to be concentrated in teaching, scientific and technical work, management or ownership of a business, and administration in a government or private bureaucracy. Eighteen respondents worked in the trades or the lower white-collar sector. Six women classified themselves as housewives. Here representativeness ends. The unknown number of francophones from Asia, Africa, and the Middle East living in Calgary were, based on my knowledge of the city's francophone community, substantially underrepresented.

The sample was a subsample of the respondents who participated in the preliminary demographic study, which was conducted by means of a mailed questionnaire (see Hébert and Stebbins 1993 for details).[6] Four hundred of the 1,200 respondents in that study who returned their questionnaires indicated their willingness to be interviewed at a later date. Sixty respondents were randomly sampled from the set of 400. When a respondent had a francophone or francophile spouse or partner, the couple was interviewed together. A significantly richer linguistic life-style in French is possible when both members can use that language. Other important details about the eight-five respondents are presented at appropriate points in chapters 3 through 8.

The primary aim of exploratory research in the social sciences is to develop grounded theory founded on a coherent set of generalizations derived from direct observations of and interviews about the object of the study. The intent of this book is to lay the foundations for a grounded theory centred on the different French language life-styles found in mid-sized and large cities where francophones live in minority circumstances. In line with this goal, I followed the usual research procedures for developing and communicating such a theory (Glaser and Strauss 1967; Strauss 1987), including two that are frequently overlooked in contemporary sociological ethnography. The first of these acknowledges that such an undertaking, when properly executed, requires the investigator to restrict substantially the presentation in research reports of descriptive material derived from the observations and interviews.[7] The second understands that, since it takes many qualitative-exploratory studies to develop such theory (see Shaffir and Stebbins 1991; Stebbins 1992a), the first study should always be viewed as a start, albeit a solid and provocative one it is hoped, rather than a decisive and final explanation of the central research problem.

Life-styles

Michael Sobel (1981: 28) concludes his review of the scattered sociological literature on life-styles with the following simple definition: Life-style is 'a distinctive, hence recognizable, mode of living.' In its simplest form a life-style consists not of a person's values, attitudes, and orientations, but of his or her routine, tangible activities (Veal 1993) as these are directly observed or deduced from observation. Among sociologists, there has been a tendency to study these activities at the individual level and, at times, to generalize from there to activities practised by entire collectivities. Sobel's definition has been used in this study, although I learned in the course of it that the interviewees commonly link certain values, attitudes, and orientations to the patterned behaviour constituting their life-styles. In everyday life it is difficult to separate the actions of people from the motives and personal meanings they use to explain and justify them (see Zurcher et al. 1971; Glyptis 1989b: 37–8).

Glyptis's (1989a: 106) review of the social science literature on life-styles turned up only a few empirical explorations. This research tends to be mainly descriptive, centring as it does on the everyday social habits of different groups and categories of people. Further, Veal (1989: 148) points out that it is fundamentally cultural in scope. That is, in this domain the investigator focuses chiefly on everyday, or ordinary, activities as they unfold within the framework of formal and informal social organization and, as I have just added, the values, attitudes, and orientations used to explain and justify these patterns.

Thus life-style research stands apart from social-structural research, the research referred to earlier as the stock-in-trade of the rather small number of sociologists who have concerned themselves over the years with the francophone communities outside Quebec. Their interests have centred on such questions as the leadership in these communities, their formal organization, governance, policies, and political and economic relations with the majority community or with other minority communities or with both (see Breton 1991 for a synthesis of Canadian research conducted from this perspective on a variety of ethnic groups). As was true for the demographic studies mentioned earlier, the present study complements the social-structural approach by sketching a portrait of francophone and francophile culture and life-style in mid-sized and large cities.[8]

This study was confined for the most part to the French-language life-styles of the respondents. On the most general plane these linguistic life-styles were found to serve the realization of four key goals held by Canadian francophones living outside Quebec: the maintenance and transmission of the French language and its associated cultures and the growth and development of individual francophones and the francophonies in which they live. This is not to argue that Franco-Calgarians and their counterparts in other Canadian cities always consciously pursue a French-language life-style for the purpose of reaching these goals, although the participants in this study did occasionally say they undertook certain activities in French precisely for such reasons. Rather it is to argue that a sizeable number of francophones and a much smaller number of francophiles are pursuing such a life-style with the result that these goals are being met to a significant degree. To streamline later discussion, the four goals will be referred to in abbreviated terms as maintenance, transmission, individual growth, and community development.

Throughout this book I speak about the plurality of francophone cultures, by which I intend to recognize their diversity in French Canada and, especially, in its urban francophonies.[9] In Calgary, for example, there are enough francophones from Quebec, Europe, Acadia, Ontario, Lebanon, Western Canada, North Africa, and South Asia to collectively sustain a reasonable number of their own distinct beliefs, values, and practices. Accordingly, francophones living in the Canadian West who were raised there consider themselves a separate cultural breed, as do francophones in other regions of the country, and they resent innocent but naive imputations by nonfrancophones that they are from Quebec or like Quebecers (Allaire 1991). Thus many events in Quebec and elsewhere in French Canada are of no special concern to these francophones, unless of course those events are seen as influencing

federal linguistic policy or in some other way affecting their linguistic existence in the West.

Nonetheless, this cultural distinctiveness should not cause us to
overlook the distaste western francophones have of being thought
of as an ethnic group. They argue, with irrefutable logic, that they
are no more an ethnic group than the country's anglophones are,
for both helped found Canada. In their minds (and in the minds
of many anglophones) they are part of one of the nation's two
charter groups, whereas immigrants from outside the country
raised to speak languages other than French are properly considered ethnic. With reference to these feelings, Bernard Bocquel
(1990: 118) argues that 'the French of the future is condemned,
if it is associated, whether closely or remotely, with an ethnic
group. French is not Ukrainian, it is not a heritage language. It is
official.' Be that as it may, I shall occasionally use the terms *ethnic*
and *ethnicity* for the convenience they afford in communicating the
perspective of sociology as applied to this area of social life.[10]

But there is another facet of lingistic life-style. The interviews
and observations demonstrate that many of Calgary's francophones
are keenly aware of the possibility of a serious loss of their capacity
to speak their mother tongue. For some of them this is of little
concern since they hope to assimilate to anglophone society in any
case. For others, however, including many of the people I interviewed, the possible loss of their mother tongue is most unsettling,
a spectre that inspires them to maintain their capacity by any
number of means, many of which they find at home. This outlook
is illustrated in the remarks of a female respondent whose marriage to an anglophone has exacerbated her problem of language
maintenance. 'I am in danger of losing my own French because of
the many years I have spent in the anglophone world. In part it is
a struggle to talk now because my own vocabulary is limited. I went
to school in English from high school on and then spoke English
only after that.' Talking with her children has become the principal avenue by which this francophone presently sustains her level
of competence in the French language.

The possibility of language loss, then, encourages many a
francophone in a city such as Calgary to seek and retain a

francophone life-style while living in an anglophone milieu as a member of a linguistic minority. Another force pushing francophones in this direction is the occasional need or desire to express one's emotions verbally. It seems that unless a person has a very good grasp of a second language he or she typically prefers the mother tongue for this kind of communication. To the extent they want to express their emotions spontaneously, whether the emotion is joy, fear, or anger, many Franco-Calgarians, my observations and interviews suggest, turn to French, or if in the company of anglophones, long to do so.

We shall see later how the preference for using one's mother tongue for emotional expression manifests itself in various everyday life situations. A female respondent who had lived in Calgary for five years following her marriage to an anglophone describes some of the complications accompanying emotional expression in a second language:

> The two cultures [anglophone and francophone] meet, from the point of view of personal communication ... especially when one wants to explain to another person in the other language from the heart, one's deep feelings, to make them understand, there is a barrier. That takes rather more time – that happens – it's rather more difficult when I explain in French things that I feel, because one has terms in each language whether in French or English that are different, that have different roots ... That takes patience on each side.

In short, the linguistic life-styles of Franco-Calgarians are grounded in the fertile soil of ethnic values and expressive communication. This study clearly demonstrates that with a few notable exceptions, the activities defining these life-styles are a fundamental part of the leisure existence of the people who lead them. This is not leisure as conventionally and narrowly defined, however, as nonobligated activity enjoyed in purely recreational circumstances unconnected with the other spheres of routine living, as is frequently true of, for example, skiing, reading, watching a film, and chatting socially with others. Rather it is leisure in the broader sense of the word – leisure as appealing, nonobligated activity found *anywhere* in the daily lives of people. Among the francophones of Calgary, leisure activities using the French language are also undertaken at home and in the volunteer world as well as in the extracurricular fringes of work and school.[11] This study suggests that it has become a central part of the life-style of the urban francophone living outside Quebec, replacing the one-time central institution of work in French, as the latter becomes increasingly difficult to find (see chapter 6). A more thorough discussion of the nature of leisure and the ways in which the various francophone leisure life-styles are pursued in Calgary will be introduced in later chapters.

As background to this discussion, however, we must first of all discover how and why over 14,400 francophones have taken up residence in Calgary, thereby constituting the largest number the city has ever known. The optimism observed in Calgary today was not always evident during the approximately 110-year history of francophone presence there.

2

From Rouleauville to Urban Francophonie

Although I have made countless trips over Route 22 to Bragg Creek, a foothills town tucked away in the southwestern exurban fringe of Calgary, it was only in recent years that I began to take seriously the small sign along the highway bearing the inscription 'Our Lady of Peace Mission Site Cairn.' Goaded by my seemingly unquenchable thirst for knowledge about the history of the French-speaking people in the region, I decided one day to make the four-kilometre drive to the west and south across the rolling prairie to a gently sloping stretch of land overlooking the Elbow River. There I learned from a stone and mortar cairn that, in 1872, Alex Cardinal had erected a crude log cabin on the site for use by two francophone Oblate priests, Constantine Scollen and Léon Doucet, as a mission for Christianizing the Indians. The mission, which is believed to be the first francophone establishment in southern Alberta, was named 'Notre Dame de la Paix.'[1]

Not long thereafter, in the summer of 1875, Father Doucet was present, forty kilometres down river from the mission at the confluence of the Bow and Elbow rivers, when Inspector Ephrem Brisebois, a Quebecer by birth, arrived with his troop of North-West Mounted Police and federal orders to establish there a fort by the name of Calgary.[2] The construction of Fort Calgary was accomplished with the aid of several Métis who were working as interpreters and bull team operators for the inspector. This French-speaking contingent was augmented in 1983–4 by a number of

cheminots, or Quebec labourers who had come west to help construct the Canadian Pacific Railway line.

The prevailing attitude at the time was one of reasonable linguistic tolerance among francophones and anglophones in a community where French-speaking whites and Métis significantly outnum-
bered the rest, all of whom spoke English. This tolerance had a
legal basis in the Northwest Territories Act of 1875, an act allowing
the use of French in the legislative council and the courts and
granting the right to establish Roman Catholic schools in which
French could be the language of instruction. In the latter half of
the 1880s, however, the linguistic ratio changed dramatically. The
number of anglophones began to increase while the number of
francophones coming from Quebec began to decline, a decline
fuelled in part by the desire of its bishops to concentrate more
exclusively on colonizing their own province. The level of tolerance
for francophones and their rights shown by the more recent anglophone migrants, some of whom were Protestant, some of whom
were Catholic, and most of whom were from Ontario, was much
lower than that of their precedessors.

The Rise and Fall of Rouleauville

With the arrival of Brisebois and the construction of Fort Calgary,
the Lady of Peace Mission (although not the log hut itself) was
shortly moved to within a couple of miles of that community and
enlarged to serve the growing francophone population gathering
there. Various Oblate priests staffed it until 1882, the year Father
Albert Lacombe arrived. In 1883, amid the influx of the cheminots
from Quebec, Father Lacombe travelled to Ottawa and, after a
great deal of wrangling with federal officials, managed to acquire
two quarter-sections of land south of, and separate from, Calgary.
On this site he set about establishing a francophone homestead
community and, to meet its religious needs, a Catholic parish that
would soon be named Notre Dame de la Paix. The streets of the
new community were laid out in gridiron fashion along the Elbow
River and for the most part given francophone names such as
Doucet and Grandin.

Lacombe dreamed of founding the 'Quebec of the West' on the banks of the Elbow. To ensure the survival of the new community he mounted a recruitment campaign in Quebec aimed at attracting residents. Few people took up the challenge, but among those who did were the Rouleau brothers. The brothers soon became prominent citizens, not only in the parish but also in the region. Charles Borromée Rouleau, who arrived in 1886, was appointed to the post of stipendiary magistrate and in the following year was selected as a judge of the Supreme Court of the Northwest Territories. Édouard Hector Rouleau joined his brother two years later to work as a surgeon for the local North-West Mounted Police detachment. Édouard also served as the Belgian consul and the first president of Calgary's St-Jean-Baptiste Society, a Quebec nationalist organization with numerous chapters throughout Canada and, at the time, parts of the United States.

In autumn 1889, in a move to achieve official recognition of their community, the homesteaders incorporated themselves as the Village of Rouleauville, named in honour of the contributions of the two brothers. It was for that period a reasonably complete community, equipped as it was with its own church, school, convent, hospital, and presbytery. But even as the village and its French name were gaining official recognition, its francophones were being overwhelmed by anglophone Irish Catholics, many of whom were most unsympathetic to any linguistic claims that might possibly threaten the standing of English.

In December 1889, the name of the parish was changed from Notre Dame de la Paix to St Mary's. Two years later a new and much larger church was built, a church that in 1913 would become the cathedral of the new Diocese of Calgary. In 1890 the church served a parish in which approximately 14 per cent spoke French as their mother tongue. Despite the heroic efforts to entice settlers from Quebec first made by Father Lacombe and later by Bishop Grandin, Parel (1987: 336) reports that by 1893 the language of the classroom and the playground at the school at Sacred Heart Convent was predominantly English. By the turn of the century 4,400 people lived in Rouleauville, slightly fewer than 3 per cent of whom were francophone (Smith 1985: 95).

Rouleauville disappeared as a corporate entity in 1907, when population pressure within the continually expanding city of Calgary forced its annexation. The hospital, the convent, and the cathedral, along with some of its associated buildings, are still in use; today they serve as a centre for Roman Catholic activities in the city. According to Robert Stamp (1980) its name continued to be printed on the city's maps until the end of the First World War. But in 1907, Rouleauville officially became just another district, just another Calgary neighbourhood. Nevertheless the new name given the district, *Mission,* immortalizes Alex Cardinal's little log hut where Father Doucet preached to the Indians thirty-five years earlier on the north bank of the Elbow River.

After Rouleauville

Father Lacombe's wish for a successful francophone parish in southern Alberta had effectively failed at least fifteen years before the annexation. Assimilation to anglophone culture had been taking place with increasing frequency since the late 1880s, a trend that was destined to continue. Yet then as now, there were members of the local francophonie who were ready to fight to retain their language and culture, justifying their actions in ways similar to those used today: The Northwest Territories Act of 1875 guaranteed certain legislative and educational rights in French. Moreover, some of those who live in minority circumstances, whatever their language and culture, have always resisted complete assimilation of another language and culture; they feel complete assimilation robs them of their very soul, because it alienates them from their maternal language and culture. Partial assimilation, which we shall see later includes certain kinds of bilingualism, allows people living in such circumstances to retain much of this ethnic heritage.

It is likely that in the wake of Rouleauville's demise, most Franco-Calgarians drifted toward complete assimilation, to such an extent that their children started life in an overwhelmingly anglophone family environment. But some Franco-Calgarians followed a different route. Competent in English, they nonetheless refused to abandon the most cherished aspects of their cultural past. The official status given to the French language in the Northwest Territories Act undoubtedly strengthened their convictions. Additionally, the vast majority of early Franco-Calgarians came from Quebec, where French was felt to be as much a part of Canadian life as English and from whence French exploration and settlement of Central and Western Canada had been conducted. They saw themselves as cofounders of Canada rather than as immigrant guests from outside. Given this belief, it would be natural for them to try to continue to live in Calgary as francophones and Quebecers, even if doing so required a special effort.

Parel (1987: 337–8) recounts how the second and third generations of Rouleaus, among others, married anglophones and through these relationships assimilated into the larger community. She also describes how people such as Victor, Adrian, and Jules Despins, who arrived from Quebec between 1910 and 1911, successfully fought complete assimilation, a feat they accomplished in part by marrying other francophones. Their children were not only fluent in French (and English) but also committed to their francophone culture.

Complete assimilation was also avoided in Calgary by francophones' working to maintain their language outside the home. For instance, in 1925 the local St-Jean-Baptiste Society, in which the Despins were active members, sought to persuade the bishop of the increasingly anglophone parish of St Mary's, Bishop Kidd, to establish a separate parish for francophones. Although he was less than sympathetic to this proposal, which he resisted by claiming the French Catholic population of Calgary was insufficiently large to justify it, he eventually capitulated, giving them permission to purchase and renovate the former Church of the Nazarene located in the Mission district, only a block from the western edge of old Rouleauville. Thus Église Sainte-Famille was officially blessed in October 1928 as a subsidiary chapel of St Mary's Cathedral, an institution that owed its existence to the private financial donations of dedicated local francophones. Along with its parish circle, which was established at about the same time (Allaire 1988: 70–3), the church would become a much-needed rallying point for Franco-

Calgarians as well as a strategic toehold in their struggle against full absorption into the anglophone world surrounding them.

A still more difficult struggle to obtain French education lay ahead. It was believed then as now that one of the most effective ways to resist complete assimilation to the anglophone world was to have all subjects taught in French at all levels of primary and secondary education. Victor Despins and Dr L.O. Beauchemin started much more modestly, however, when in 1933 they approached the Catholic school board, asking for an improvement in the quality and an increase in the amount of French instruction throughout the system. As the two men realized, full French instruction was out of the question, since both the St Mary's girls and boys' schools in Rouleauville in the late nineteenth and early twentieth centuries, as well as their predecessor, the little convent school at Sacred Heart, had always offered only part of their curricula in that language. Moreover, a series of repressive measures had been enacted in many parts of English Canada during the same period, one effect of which was to place severe legal restrictions on French-language instruction there (Office of the Commissioner of Official Languages 1988: 1175).

Not surprisingly, their request was denied, not only in 1933 but again five years later when they decided to ask for a French school. On these and other occasions, the answer always resembled the one given by Bishop Kidd: the city had too few francophone children to justify approving such a proposal. This reasoning is still heard in parts of Alberta as well as in many other regions of Canada outside Quebec where francophones are trying to counteract full assimilation by gaining control of their children's education.[3]

Franco-Calgarians had to wait until after the Second World War to obtain a significant level of instruction in French, which was then introduced in the Catholic junior high schools. Meanwhile an entire generation, in struggling to preserve its heritage, was forced to rely on the Calgary public schools, schools where French was taught only in language classes designed for anglophone students. For that generation the alternative was most unpleasant: the children had to be sent to a residential school, usually one in

Quebec, Edmonton, or Gravelbourg, Saskatchewan (Collège Mathieu). The financial and emotional costs of this solution were enormous, even if this response did convincingly demonstrate the intensity with which certain, usually wealthy, Calgary francophones valued their cultural heritage.

The Oil Boom

The opening of the junior high school program might have been delayed even longer had oil not been discovered in 1947 at Leduc, Alberta. One consequence of this was the phenomenal development of the province's petroleum industry. Calgary became the administrative centre of the industry and the new home of a number of French-speaking immigrants whose professional qualifications were in high demand. The largest contingent of immigrants came from Belgium and France during the 1950s, bringing an intense desire for French education for their children and in many instances French Catholicism for the entire family. As the population of Franco-Calgarians increased, the justification for separate French schools based on numbers became more convincing.

This population increase was having a similar effect in the area of religion. Not only did the call for a separate parish become louder, but also the number of people who were prepared to pledge money toward the construction of a new and larger church grew. At midnight on Christmas Eve, 1963, Église Sainte-Famille celebrated its first mass in its new building, the building still used today for religious services and religious and social functions related to the parish and the wider francophone community. The event also marked the inauguration of an independent French parish in Calgary, ending the classification of 'subsidiary chapel' granted thirty years earlier. Not long afterward Église Sainte-Famille was placed under the jurisdiction of the Oblate Fathers of Alberta; French Catholic religious governance in Calgary had come full circle.

The Era of Official Bilingualism

The year 1969 was a turning-point in the history of linguistic relations in Canada. That year the federal policy of official bilingualism was put into effect; its two main goals were to help anglophones and francophones living in minority circumstances transmit and maintain their languages and associated cultures. These goals were to be reached in part by institutionalizing both French and English as working languages in Parliament, the federal civil service, the Canadian Broadcasting Corporation/La Société Radio-Canada, and the various government departments and administrative agencies. The Department of the Secretary of State was in charge of implementing the policy, while the newly created Commissioner of Official Languages, who was responsible to parliament, monitored the progress of bilingualism across the country.

In 1988, a new federal law on official languages gave the Department of the Secretary of State two additional goals to pursue. These were: 'enhancing the vitality of the English and French linguistic minority communities in Canada and supporting and assisting their development and fostering the full recognition and use of both English and French in Canadian society' (Commissioner of Official Languages 1989: 63). In other words the Secretary of State gained several additional responsibilities – to promote, extend, and improve the teaching of English and French in minority circumstances and to encourage 'the business community, labour organizations, voluntary organizations and other organizations or institutions to provide services in both English and French and to foster the recognition and use of those languages' (Commissioner of Official Languages 1989: 66). In practice this meant promoting the development of various French and English cultural institutions operating in minority circumstances, including community clubs, radio stations, newspapers, networks, events, and festivals.

The passage and implementation of the second Official Languages Act left no doubt that the federal government was in effect pursuing the same four goals served by the life-styles of urban francophones in Canada: the maintenance and transmission of the French language and its associated cultures and the growth and development of individual francophones and the francophonies in which they live. Implementation of the policy of official bilingualism and its revisions has substantially affected the franco-phones and francophiles of Calgary and their counterparts in other Canadian cities outside Quebec (cf., Savas 1991: 68).[4] In particular it has left its mark on educational and organizational life, coming as it did at a time when the Catholic church could no longer support these institutions at the level it had in the past.

Education

For many decades the demands of Franco-Calgarians for adequate education in French have been publicly expressed, along with similar demands made by other Franco-Albertans, by the Association Canadienne-Française de l'Alberta (ACFA). ACFA has worked from its inception in 1926 to promote the collective social, cultural, political, and economic interests of the province's francophones, one of the most critical being French-language education. Under pressure from ACFA and later the Official Languages Acts and Article 23 of the Charter of Rights and Freedoms (1982), the Government of Alberta began to consider more seriously claims such as those made by Despins and Beauchemin in the 1930s and 1940s.

Smith (1985: 104) reports that the provincial government changed the School Act in 1964 to allow any school board in Alberta to authorize the use of French as well as English as the language of instruction in grades one through eight, and after 1968 in grades nine through twelve. Such instruction could account for up to 50 per cent of all instruction in bilingual schools. Before this, in schools where French-speaking students were enrolled, the use of French was limited to approximately one hour a day starting with grade two. In 1976 the government authorized French immersion schools and in 1984, two years after ratification of the new Canadian Constitution, all-French schools (where all subjects are taught in French except for English) were permitted to operate under the aegis of the Calgary and Edmonton Catholic school boards.[5]

Franco-Calgarians wasted little time once these changes were proclaimed. By 1969 the pressure from both anglophone and francophone parents was sufficient to force the Catholic school system in Calgary to launch its own bilingual program. In September 1984, following government authorization of all-French schools, the Calgary Catholic School Board opened École Sainte-Anne (known in its first year as École Saint-Antoine), the first school of this kind in southern Alberta. It served students from kindergarten (the maternelle) through grade nine until 1989 when, owing to a substantial increase in demand for instruction in French and the addition of more advanced grades, it was reorganized. The new institution now offers grades four through twelve, as well as kindergarten and grades one through three at its subsidiary, Pavillon Saint-Paul.

According to the 1991 edition of ACFA's directory, or *Annuaire*, Calgary francophones now have access not only to a complete system of primary and secondary education in French, but also to three French-language preschools (the prématernelles) and three bilingual or all-French day-care centres (the garderies). In 1993–4 École Sainte-Anne (including Pavillon Saint-Paul) enrolled 434 students, an enrolment that represents a steady but modest annual increase dating from the inception of all-French schools in the city.[6] This figure might be higher were the school more accessible to some of the parents and were it as well-equipped as the larger (English) schools.

We shall see in chapter 4 that Franco-Calgarians have generally patronized either the all-French schools or the immersion schools of the Calgary Catholic School Board or, more rarely, the immersion or the all-English schools of the Calgary School Board in the public system. There were and still are, however, other all-French schools in the city to which a small proportion of its francophones have sent or now send their children. For example, the French petrochemical firm Aquitaine ran a school for the children of its employees from 1966 through 1972, part of the period during which it maintained offices in Calgary. Student papers and examinations were sent to France for correction.[7] The Lycée Louis Pasteur, which is part of a world-wide network of more than 450 schools, established a Calgary school in 1982 and continues to offer an all-French preschool and all-French instruction through the equivalent of grade nine. Although it is a small private institution, it nonetheless helps meet the substantial demand in the city for French education. Another private institution, the Calgary French School, offers a Canadian-based immersion program for students from kindergarten through grade nine.

In general, the history of French-language education in Calgary has been a history of a deeply felt, two-pronged mission by its francophones: to establish French educational programs and to gain control of their administration. Even before Rouleauville passed from the scene, anglophone Catholics had taken over the responsibility of educating francophone Catholics in French. We shall see that only late in 1993 did Franco-Albertans finally gain control of their own programs, even though some of them had managed to establish those programs somewhat earlier, as did the francophones of Calgary.

Organizations

Although ACFA had been active in Calgary and throughout Alberta since 1926, francophone organizational life in the city really blossomed with the proclamation of the Official Languages Act of 1969 and even more so after the passage of the 1988 Act. It is true that some clubs and associations predate the latter, including the Société Franco-Canadienne de Calgary, a volunteer-service organization dedicated to helping the local francophonie in a number of key areas; the Gigueurs de Calgary, a traditional dance troupe; and the Voix des Rocheuses, an a cappella chorus. The first was founded in 1970, the second two in 1978. Yet many of Calgary's francophone organizations have come into existence only in recent years in response to an expanding range of francophone needs. Indeed their number has grown to the point where it has become necessary to coordinate their activities, a community need that has been met by the Société du Centre Scolaire Communautaire de Calgary since its establishment in early 1993. In April that same year the Table de Concertation Régionale was established to identify the priorities held in common by several of the organizations and to encourage their collaboration toward the realization of these priorities. A number of these organizations will be considered in detail in chapter 6. What is of concern in the present chapter is the history of francophone organizational life in Calgary.

Between the demise of Rouleauville and the institution of federal funding for the organizational and cultural activities of the two official linguistic minorities, organized social life among Calgary francophones, so far as I can tell from the little history available on the matter, centred mostly on Église Sainte-Famille, its parish circle, the Société Saint-Jean-Baptiste (founded in 1888), and the Club Français (founded in 1919). The latter two continued to function until 1970, when they were amalgamated under the name of the Société Franco-Canadienne de Calgary (Bertrand 1993: 6). As the opportunity grew from the 1960s onward for schooling in French, so did the formal organization of community social life, because the schools themselves became new rallying points, including most recently the preschools and day-care centres. Before the advent of formal French schooling, however, one can only speculate that the informal world was also active, as manifested in the networks of family and friends whose activities must have helped sustain the francophone world of the city at times and places beyond the scope of the church and the formal associations.

Parel (1987) mentions the activities of the local St-Jean-Baptiste Society, possibly the most dynamic francophone voluntary organization in its day. But it appears that its influence in Calgary began to wane significantly in the mid-1920s, when ACFA took over as the province-wide champion of francophone interests (Smith 1985: 100) and the home office of the society in Quebec began to redirect its attention away from francophone problems outside Quebec to those within (Jones 1988: 1913). It may be that at this time the curé and his parishioners at Église Sainte-Famille and the members of the Club Français and the St-Jean-Baptiste Society entered into a more equal sharing of the various formally organized local social functions. They continued in this relationship until the number of lay organizations began to proliferate in the 1970s and 1980s.

Two Worlds: Formal and Informal

One of the lessons contained in this brief history of the Calgary francophonie is that the community's survival through the years has depended on a complex interweaving of formal organizations (clubs, churches, schools, associations) and informal social arrangements (friendships, family relationships, interpersonal networks, social gatherings). The contribution of the informal world to the survival of francophone life in the city has been largely ignored in the written histories I have consulted, quite possibly because it is so much more difficult to study historically. Organizations usually leave records; social relationships usually do not. One might interview community old-timers about the latter, but the very informality of social life leaves its participants with few memorable events around which to organize recall at a later date.

Despite the organizational richness of the 1990s, the Calgary French community passed through a long period of organizational poverty, starting around the beginning of this century with the decline of Rouleauville and ending in the 1960s with the influx of French-speaking immigrants whose numbers helped justify a new church and French-language schooling. During the intervening years, organizational life, according to the historical sources used here, appears to have been too underdeveloped to sustain the francophonie on its own. Yet the local francophones soldiered on, developing an informal world sufficiently solid to support itself and the formal world and carry forward the rudiments of a francophone life-style, so that a foundation was available in the early 1960s on which both locals and immigrants could build and expand.

Another aspect of social life almost entirely overlooked by the histories of the Calgary francophone community is its sporadic internal conflicts. Some mention of certain external conflicts is made in the histories, chiefly the conflict with the provincial authorities over the right to education in French. Yet both the interviews and the many casual conversations held during the observations of this study revealed significant internal tension in the 1960s and later, as francophone immigrants from Europe differed with their Canadian counterparts on key issues, and the latter differed among themselves on still other issues. Some of this conflict took place and is still taking place in the informal world. It probably took place before 1960 as well, but I have met few people who have been around Calgary long enough to know about it.

By way of illustration let us consider the following paraphrase of what one respondent referred to as la grande chicane (the great squabble), a community-wide conflict in the 1970s that embraced both its formal and informal segments:

The Calgary French community was split in the 1970s by a major dispute centred, in part, on the linguistic differences separating the francophones from France and those from Quebec and other regions of Canada. Many of those from France were employed by Aquitaine. They dominated Calgary's representation to the ACFA, whereas the French Canadians rallied around the Société Franco-Canadienne de Calgary. The Alliance Française was, at the time, very much guided by Paris; it reflected the low opinion of Parisians toward the quality of Quebec French. At stake in the dispute was the quality of French education in Calgary. Many francophones, weary of the squabble, began to abandon the local francophonie, which meant they had to face gradual assimilation into the anglophone world. The dispute started to subside in the late 1970s, in part because Aquitaine left Calgary. More recently the Alliance Française has become more friendly to French Canadians and their culture and language. Also many francophones of many different origins have begun to rally around the recent school-community centre project [discussed in chapter 9].

We shall see later that conflicting views on the quality of Canadian French are still heard from time to time on the informal level.

As the present study strongly suggests, the complex interweaving of the formal and informal worlds, whether conflictual or consensual, is still very important, still very much a part of the social existence of all French Canadians living outside Quebec, still very much a part of the realization of the four goals. Nevertheless, the tendency to underestimate the role and impact of the informal world persists, among both the local francophones and the social scientists who study them. The examination of francophone life-styles can help correct this analytic imbalance, because the concept of life-style automatically leads us to consider both worlds as well as their intricate interrelationship and relative importance. Within this framework we must consider both external and internal conflict, since the pursuit of major collective goals inevitably generates some discord. There are bound to be different blueprints for the pursuit of the 'good life.'

Let us turn first to the core of the informal world of the Calgary francophonie – the linguistic life-styles led by its parents and their children.

3

Parents, Children, and French

Whether the mother tongue is French or English, family and household composition varies enormously in the typical Canadian city. Some people live alone; some live with one or more friends; some cohabit with another person; some are married but have no children. Where there are children they may be part of a family with a mother and a father – what most people think of as a 'family' – part of a family with only one parent, or part of a family made up of one or more extended relatives. For francophones in a city such as Calgary, family and household composition substantially influences the ways they retain their fluency in French, grow as francophone persons, and participate in the affairs of the local francophonie.

In other words, both inside and outside the home the composition of a person's family and household helps shape his or her linguistic life-style as a child and as an adult. Although this condition is examined most extensively in this chapter and the next two, it reappears in one way or another in all the remaining chapters of the book. Family and household composition are among the most important ways in which the informal world affects the realization of the francophone's goals of maintenance, transmission, personal growth, and community development.

The Family Circle

Since I encountered very few single-parent families during the interviews, discussion here is confined to families created from three main types of marriage according to language: the all-French endogamous marriage (francophone-francophone, francophone-francophile), the type-1 French-English exogamous marriage (female francophone–male nonfrancophone), and type-2 French-English exogamous marriage (male francophone–female nonfrancophone). The nonfrancophones were usually anglophone, although a few of them who routinely spoke English were reported by their spouses to have as their mother tongue a language other than French or English. I interviewed both members of twelve endogamous couples (n = 24); three of these were composed of a francophone and a francophile. In addition, I interviewed fourteen women in type-1 exogamous relationships and four men in type-2 exogamous relationships (the non-French speaking partners in these couples were not interviewed).

The study sought information from couples with and without children for each type of marriage. Altogether, forty-four of the eighty-five respondents had children; in some instances they were now adult and living away from home. Some of the forty-four men and women were widowed, divorced, or separated at the time of the interviews, but they too had once raised children in an exogamous or endogamous relationship.

Whether a marriage is endogamous or exogamous, the family activities undertaken in French with the children are much the same. Important differences become evident, however, when we explore the three types of marriages to discover who participates in the activities and what conditions govern that participation.

Home Activities

Like so much of everyday life, the activities conducted at home in French are simple. They are not, however, trivial, if for no other reason than that they move both children and adults closer to realizing the goals of maintenance, transmission, personal growth and, indirectly, community development. How effective these activities are is largely determined by the intimacy and familiarity of the surroundings, the relationships of those carrying out the activities, as well as by their frequency. Their intimacy, simplicity, and familiarity are what makes them attractive, and what establishes them as part of the core of the informal francophone world of Calgary.

The activities described here are carried out, usually separately, by one or both parents, with one or more of their children. First, there is the set of activities in which one parent performs, as it were, to an audience of one or more of his or her children, typically by reading stories, telling tales, singing lullabies, and reciting nursery rhymes. These early experiences in French, which are sometimes expanded when the child recites a French prayer at bedtime, combine to form an initial, positive, three-way emotional bond linking the child with the French language and the parent involved. At this point, the child starts down the long road leading to mastery of his or her mother tongue in an atmosphere of love and warmth created by a mother or father who routinely provides nurturance and pleasurable experiences.

Many francophone parents said they had little choice but to conduct these activities in French, however eager they were to transmit their mother tongue to their children. When they were young, their parents had raised them in similar ways with stories and tales; many years later these were still known to them only in French. Even if, in their adult lives, they learned the English versions of some of these, the positive emotional loading acquired during the intimacy of their own childhood has permanently endowed the French versions with a very special appeal.

The tales, stories, and prayers are told and retold over the years as the child grows older, but the lullabies and nursery rhymes are soon replaced with activities in French that he or she initiates. The child's initiative is augmented by parental encouragement and sometimes parental insistence, leading him or her to read in French, listen to recorded French songs, or watch a children's program on French television. It is possible in Calgary to rent French videotapes and audio recordings for adults and children. Children's books, videotapes, and audio recordings in French can also be purchased at the local French bookstore, La Ruelle, or borrowed from the public or French and immersion school libraries. Catalogues from two Quebec mail-order houses selling videotapes and books for adults and children circulate in Calgary. Moreover, parents often buy such items while on business and pleasure trips to Quebec or Europe. Commercial and homemade videotapes sent by friends and relatives in Quebec, France, and elsewhere expand still further this pool of learning resources.

Occupation with these different everyday practices leaves preschool children in all-French families with relatively little contact in English, an arrangement that certainly helps their parents prevent English-language interests from creeping in and taking over. The involvement of the children with anglophone playmates in the neighborhood appears to have no significant effect on their commitment to the French language and its associated culture. Life's most important activities at this point in their lives are family activities, which for francophone children take place in a French milieu.[1]

Depending on the linguistic composition of the family, a conspicuous French auditory and visual environment can complement the verbal Frenchness of the home. Many of the francophone parents in this study read French books, watch French television, listen to French vocal music, or subscribe to French magazines and newspapers, and many do more than one of these. Although this is hardly fare for preschool children, its presence in the home enhances their sense of the place as being French in some important measure. French posters, calendars, announcements, advertisements, and similar decorations can also add significantly to the domestic culture.

With the growth of their child's verbal and intellectual capacity, most francophone parents reported that he or she became interested in games played in French and in singing French songs with other members of the family.[2] In addition, many of the francophone respondents, whether in endogamous or exogamous relationships, regularly converse by long-distance telephone with their parents, brothers and sisters, and possibly other relatives. Respondents with children said that it is important for them to speak French, if for no other reason than to be able to talk with their parents (the children's grandparents) who frequently speak little or no English. For their part, grandparents in particular were said to be eager to encourage competency in French in their grandchildren; this they did by sending them books, videotapes, vocal recordings, or a subscription to a children's magazine, all in French.

Family Activities Outside the Home

Not all family activities take place inside the home. During external activities, francophone parents (and some francophile parents), eager as they are to establish and maintain French language competence in their children, seize every opportunity that comes along to continue their communication en français. They recognize the fragility of the position of French language in Calgary and adhere to the commonsense principle that the more their children hear, read, and speak French, the less likely they are to lose it later in the teen-age and young adult years of high susceptibility to the often irresistible appeal of the English language and anglophone popular culture.

A small number of organized French activities are routinely available in the city for preschool children. Perhaps the best known of these are those arranged by the Copains de Jeux. This informal group of sixty children and their parents, founded in 1988, meets regularly for the purpose of stimulating the use of French in contexts appealing to both (a play session at a park, a trip to the zoo, an hour at a swimming pool). The Alliance Française arranges similar sessions for parents and their preschool children under the name of 'Allo Maman?' Additionally, certain branch libraries offer scheduled readings of French stories for children. Parents, usually mothers, participate with their children in these activities (which is why they are treated here as an aspect of family life).[3]

Likewise, any occasion outside the home where parents and children are free to speak together in French can become still another opportunity to reinforce the special linguistic bond that has developed between them. These occasions are many and varied. Parents and children speak French to one another while shopping; indeed, the different experiences in the marketplace aid the development of vocabulary. Although many of the respondents were not members of Église Sainte-Famille, those who were rely on certain church functions to help keep French alive in the minds of their children. Finally, a number of leisure activities encourage talk – in this case French talk – about the activity itself and the surroundings in which it unfolds. The interviewees particularly mentioned that family skating, skiing, hiking, camping, picnicking, tobogganing, and dining together at restaurants generated lively conversations in French.

Family Composition

We noted earlier that these activities are carried out in all families, whether founded on an endogamous or an exogamous marriage. But in the two types of exogamous marriage the activities conducted in French vary according to the sex of the parent who participates in them with the child, the frequency with which that parent can conduct a particular activity in French, and the amount of time he or she can speak French while engaging in the activity. The use of French at home is simplest in families created by two francophones united in an endogamous marriage.

The Endogamous Marriage

It is clear from this study that when both parents are francophone or one is a francophone and the other a fluent francophile, the language of the household is predominantly, and in a few instances, exclusively French. Accordingly, the children in these families spend their infant and preschool years in a solidly French domestic environment in which there is no real competing language. Still, it is true that the large majority of the francophones interviewed for this study also speak English and that they occasionally speak it at home where their children hear them. At times it is simply more efficient in the rushed urban world in which parents live these days to discuss certain everyday events and problems in English. A male francophone who works in English described some of the problems he faces in this regard: 'I work in

English, and then when I want to talk to [my wife] about it in French I realize that I lack the vocabulary to do this. It often happens that we end up talking in English about my work even though we generally speak French here at home.' When discussing together an English realty contract, operating manual, or newspaper article, for example, it makes little sense to talk about it in French when the couple can read and speak English. It is also possible that, even though they are francophones, they lack the French vocabulary to discuss certain technical matters they have come to know only in English.

Notwithstanding this general tendency to occasionally favor the ideal of efficiency over that of the linguistic purity of the home, a small number of francophone families in Calgary (except when they are in the company of anglophones), assiduously strive to keep English out of all domestic and public talk. For truly bilingual parents this can be more challenging than one might think, for they are sometimes unaware of which language they are using. These parents commonly work and shop in English, but use French at home and in many of their leisure activities. They are so fluent in the two languages that they sometimes speak at home in English even when they have intended to speak in French.

Meanwhile, children sometimes want to speak English at home, usually because they can express themselves better in English when dealing with certain subjects, they prefer it to French, or being bilingual themselves, they are unaware of which language they are using. The irony in all this is that their bilingual parents may not realize that their child is using English and as a result talk with him or her for several minutes in the forbidden tongue. Thus even those parents with the greatest determination to keep the household exclusively French occasionally lose control and allow some English to invade.

Finally, even if domestic discourse takes place *almost* exclusively in French, some other facets of home life clearly do not. Calgary has only one, and in some parts of the city two, French television channels and only one French radio station. They must compete with over thirty English channels and over twenty English stations. When it comes to language, the children of the interviewees are rarely denied their choice of radio and television programs or their choice of recreational reading. Moreover, in many households anglophone friends phone regularly, shattering the all-French ambiance with English chatter, if an ongoing English television sitcom has not already achieved the same effect. Some parents even subscribe to English-language newspapers and magazines; these lie around the house as stark reminders of the bustling anglophone world on the other side of the walls.

A particularly difficult problem for Calgary francophones and francophiles who want to protect their home environment from incursions of English is finding baby sitters who can speak French. Good babysitters are difficult enough to find without adding the requirement of language. They are chosen for their proximity, their reliability, their moral integrity, their ability to get along with the children, among other criteria. Finding a sitter who meets these criteria and speaks French as well is no small challenge. Apart from proximity, perhaps, these specifications cannot be sacrificed, which means that for the sample as a whole, frequent compromises were made when it came to the sitter's linguistic qualifications. Such compromises can encourage assimilation to the wider culture when parents frequently use anglophone sitters and when, admiring their sitters, their children imitate them. Nevertheless, the willingness of many respondents to search at length for a French-speaking gardien (sometimes even to serve full-time during the work week) and to provide transportation for one who lives in another part of town, demonstrates their dedication to the goals of maintenance, transmission, and personal development.

I did encounter a family in the course of the study where the parents had succeeded much more than the other parents in keeping *all* things anglophone out of the home and the lives of their two children. These parents subscribed strictly to francophone periodicals and permitted only French radio and television. The children attended French schools until grade nine, after which they had no alternative at the time but to enrol in a bilingual institution. Their parents also engineered most of their social contacts so that they associated largely with francophones. Religious services and other events at Église Sainte-Famille, for example, facilitated pursuit of this goal. Yet despite all this the two children learned English well enough at school (especially at the bilingual institution) and around the neighbourhood to gain entry to an anglophone university and perform admirably at their studies there.

The Exogamous Marriage

Fourteen of the exogamous marriages in this study were type 1, the remaining four were type 2. The interviews with the francophones in these relationships strongly suggest that their children are much more likely to develop a facility in French and a commitment to the language and culture of the francophone parent when that parent is their mother, a finding that is in accord with recent national studies on the matter (Churchill and Kaprielian-Churchill 1991: 48; *Le Chaînon* 1993: 2; Turcotte 1993: 17). As a general rule the mothers in the families contacted in this study, whether anglophone or francophone, whether employed outside the home or not, appeared to spend a significantly greater amount of time with their children than the fathers, especially when the children were young.

This close relationship gives the mothers a singular advantage in inculcating their first language, an advantage which by the way the francophile mothers in this study did not use. Instead they spoke their second language – French – with their children much, if not all, of the time. The anglophone mothers, by contrast, had no choice but to speak English, although it seems they regretted this limitation. When interviewed, their husbands said that their anglophone wives shared their desire to raise their children as bilingual francophones. All four mothers were trying to learn French, and all had enthusiastically planned to send their children either to a French school or to an immersion school.

Linguistic problems were most evident in the families founded on type-1 exogamous marriages (see also Heller and Lévy 1992: 11–3). Here the mothers had to a significant degree succeeded, or were in the process of succeeding in raising their children as francophones, at least up to the teen-age years. But according to the evidence presented in the interviews, the anglophone fathers were a constant hindrance to this mission, for they were generally less sympathetic toward French in general, and French in their home in particular, than the anglophone mothers were. It is true that all the anglophone fathers had accepted their partners' wishes to send their children to French schools, when they might have reached a compromise on an immersion school or insisted on an English school. But only one anglophone father was said to have a genuine commitment to learning French, and very few fathers took an interest in the bilingual activities of the local francophonie (see chapter 8).

Faced with this attitude, the francophone mothers uniformly concluded they must tackle 'the French question' with diplomacy (or politeness, as some of them put it), whereas the francophone fathers never mentioned the need for such an approach with their anglophone wives. In practical terms, the need to be diplomatic means that francophone mothers must try to speak largely, if not exclusively, in English with the children when their father is present so he can participate in the interaction, however brief it may be. One francophone mother observed: 'when my family from Quebec visits us we have to speak in English when he [her husband] is around even though he is the only one in the room who cannot understand French. If we do not he gets upset.' Another mother with one preschool child discussed a different problem: 'Since my husband is anglophone we talk nearly all the time in English. Although he can understand French to some extent, it is much easier to deal with the problems of everyday life in English. With both of us working there is enough stress without adding language difficulties.' In short, for families founded on type-1 exogamous marriages French talk is apt to be limited to those occasions when the francophone mother is alone with her children.

Diplomacy and compromise reach their maximum expression in naming children. In the mixed marriages of this study, children had to be given names with which members of the extended families of both parents could identify. Their names also had to be pronounceable in both languages, with minimal variation between the two languages in pronunciation. Furthermore, the names had to have a modern 'ring' to them in contemporary francophone and anglophone society. With a few exceptions these rules of naming were followed.

But faithful adherence to such rules meant that the number of remaining names from which to choose was, for some respondents, surprisingly small. Nevertheless those chosen (Paul, Marc, Philippe, Julie, Mélanie, and Stéphanie) were regarded by their parents as the solution to a potentially thorny family problem, particularly with reference to the grandparents who were sometimes less than enthusiastic about the cross-language marriage itself. One respondent described the persistent difficulty his parents, brothers, and sisters had with Jason, his son's name, explaining that: 'In French the pronunciation is quite different. Moreover it is extremely rare to meet someone in Quebec whose name is Jason. As a result my relatives always have difficulty when they refer to him by his name [points to the baby in his mother's arms]. We never thought about such complications when we chose the name.'

All the exchanges between the parents in the exogamous marriages were carried out in English, a practice that significantly affected the linguistic atmosphere of the home. Most of the respondents in these marriages, when asked to classify all the talk done at home, estimated that English was spoken 75 to 80 per cent of the time. Nonetheless the francophone mothers spoke proudly about how they persevered at keeping French alive as the language of communication with their children. As indicated earlier, they did this by being tenacious, and by refusing to interact with them unless addressed in French (that is unless their own fluency in English led them to respond inadvertently in that language).

In sum, the domestic part of the linguistic life-style of francophone parents in mixed marriages is founded chiefly on their relationships with their children. 'The dominant language around here,' one mother noted, 'is English. I speak in French with my children, but that is all.' Another observed that: 'my only chance to use my French at home is in talking with my children. Of course I read some in French and watch some French television, but speaking it, well, there are no other opportunities unless my relatives or francophone friends visit us.'

Conclusion

From this picture of the domestic side of the francophone lifestyle, and especially the part portraying the exogamous marriage, one might reasonably conclude that the four goals of the francophonie are unlikely to be reached in the next generation. Such a pessimistic conclusion is consistent with the results of the demographic survey conducted by Roger Bernard (1991) for the Fédération des Jeunes Canadiens Français. He found, as we have here, that children of exogamous marriage are somewhat more likely to use French at home when their mother is francophone than when their father is francophone. He also found that by age six only 45.1 per cent of the children whose mothers were francophone were still speaking with them in French, a proportion that drops to 36.5 per cent by age thirteen. The proportion of those speaking in French with a francophone father and with siblings at these ages were even lower. These figures are in accord with data from the 1971 and 1991 censuses which show that outside Quebec the proportion of the Canadian population using French in the home has declined by nearly half, dropping from 4.3 to 2.2 per cent (Statistics Canada 1984:8; Statistics Canada 1993: 10–11). Exogamous marriages are often cited as a main force behind this decline; outside Quebec they constitute over 70 per cent of all marriages composed of one or two francophones (*Le Chaînon* 1992: 5).[4]

Yet pessimistic conclusions may be premature, for parents have many resources at their disposal with which to combat their own and their children's complete assimilation to anglophone culture. Parental determination appears to be a key force in all this; francophone parents recognize they have a challenge before them, but are determined to meet it as best they can. In doing so, many of them have shown a remarkable inventiveness in the ways they incorporate French into their own lives and the lives of their offspring. For instance, in their search for things to do in French with their children, some parents have either discovered or created some rather unusual projects and activities, compared with what one might observe in the typical anglophone family in North America. These projects and activities include playing charades, singing with the family, doing cross-word puzzles, editing a family newspaper, and maintaining a scrapbook of clippings. What is more, such projects and activities invite the children and their francophone parents to be active participants in the linguistic socialization of the children and sometimes even the parents. This contrasts with the more passive life-style of many anglophone children and made possible by the copious amounts of English television available to them.

For all its problems, the family continues to be the most important arena of francophone activities for the preschool child and one of the most important for school-aged children. The various activities outside the home organized by certain external agencies can add significantly to this base. In Calgary these activities, although relatively few in number, nevertheless play an important supplementary role in promoting the French language and its associated francophone culture.

4

Francophone Children in the Community

The focus on children here might suggest that we have lost sight of the main theme of this book, namely, the linguistic life-styles of adult francophones and francophiles in Calgary. Although children are not our the primary object of study, it must be acknowledged that they do affect the life-style of their parents in many important ways and therefore can hardly be ignored. The intimate francophone family activities in which children participate with their parents help the latter reach the community goals of maintenance, transmission, and personal development. When the children are old enough to circulate on their own in the larger francophonie, their parents also benefit from the contacts they make there, since they commonly become involved in some way as well.

The children's contacts with the wider francophone community are made through two basic types of activities: educational and extracurricular. The first refers to the activities taking place during school hours, as well as those taking place after school hours under the aegis of the institution. The second refers to the activities in a child's life with no direct connection to the school. Since no children were interviewed or systematically observed in this study, little can be said here about their view of their educational and extracurricular experiences. Rather, our concern will be with their parents' involvement in these activities and how this involvement has shaped their linguistic life-styles as adults living in an anglophone city.

Educational Activities

From interviews with both parents and couples planning to have children, I learned that the most common preference for schooling was overwhelmingly that offered in the all-French system. Only a handful of couples – all of them francophone – diverged from this pattern, preferring instead either the immersion schools or the English schools. Slightly under two-thirds of the mixed couples were, or would be sending their children to a French school, whereas the others were, or would be sending them to an immersion school.[1] The preference for all-French schooling among both endogamous and exogamous couples was more pronounced for the second child than for the first. The average number of children per parent was 2.1.

To be eligible to send a child to École Sainte-Anne, at least one parent must be francophone and Roman Catholic and have received his or her primary or secondary education in French. A small number of exceptions to this religious condition are granted to francophone immigrants. The preference for all-French schooling in itself demonstrates the considerable commitment many respondents have to the French language and francophone culture. Moreover, it was by referring to this commitment that they frequently defended their choice of school. Several parents explained that their children would learn to speak French well at École Sainte-Anne, because they would be in the company of francophone peers, whereas at an immersion school they would develop an English accent from emulating anglophone friends.[2] Moreover, they said, the children would learn more about the francophone cultures of the world than they would were they to attend any other kind of school. A few of the respondents believed, however, that to gain access to the range of facilities and opportunities made possible by a substantially greater number of students, they might ultimately have to send their children to one of the large all-English or French immersion high schools or to a large private French school in another city. In the experience of one interviewee in this study, a significant number of students do leave École Sainte-Anne for this reason.

For the children, entry into the world of French formal education adds considerably to their list of francophone activities, which
up to this point was almost exclusively family-related. The centrality
of school in their lives is immediately felt at home, particularly by
those there who speak French. Like many other North American
parents, these parents reported spending a great deal of time
discussing homework assignments, relationships with teachers and
classmates, and the important events of the day. This kind of talk,
which is carried out in French whenever possible, continues
throughout the school year. In addition, the parents attend occasional parent-teacher meetings about the academic progress of
their child as well as school-wide meetings concerning the educational plans and policies of the institution.

Volunteer work constitutes still another francophone activity
available to Franco-Calgarians through the schools. As a number
of respondents observed, this turns out to be a good way to meet
other francophones and to find other parents with whom to establish a car pool for transporting their children to and from school.
With only one French school serving a catchment area encompass-
ing the entire city, an undeniable need for car pooling exists.
Somewhat over half the respondents with children in school spent
a portion of their free time as school volunteers, sometimes as
classroom aids, sometimes as helpers at sports events and science
fairs, sometimes as members or officers of the school's parents'
committee (*comité de parents*). The role of president of the parents'
committee is especially time consuming. One female respondent
whose exogamous marriage had resulted in three children, all of
whom were attending or were destined to attend the city's French
schools, described her work as a volunteer and president of one of
these committees as follows: 'I was president of the parents' committee of [a preschool]; this required a considerable amount of
time. You know, you are responsible for everything in such a position. But that is not all that I have done for the schools. I volunteer two or three times a week in helping the pupils with their
reading. I also help in some way when there is a sports tourna-
ment.' This woman's record of helping at school was exceptional
when compared with that of most of the other respondents with

school-age children. Some of those others, however, did volunteer, sometimes extensively, in other spheres of francophone life in the city (see chapter 6).

Parents' committees are unique to the French communities of Manitoba and Alberta, where they play a distinctly different role from the Parent-Teachers and Canadian Home and School Associations found in anglophone educational circles throughout North America. These committees, whose members are elected from among the parents of the children attending a particular school, are one of the important organizational responses of francophones in Manitoba and Alberta to the right given to both official language groups by the Canadian Charter of Rights and Freedoms – that is, the right to educate their children in French or English when one or the other is the first language of one or both parents. That is, it is the first language the parents learned and still understand or the language in which they received their primary school instruction. In Alberta, parents' committees work with school administrations to ensure the implementation of this right and the provision of an acceptable quality of French education for the students. They support and participate in the educational and extracurricular activities of the schools, and in this manner help them reach these goals. By 1992, thirty-three such committees had been established in Alberta under the direction of an overarching provincial federation, La Fédération des Parents Francophones de l'Alberta.

In addition to the previously mentioned involvements, the parents in this study talked about the contact they occasionally had through their childrens' schools with francophone élite and popular culture. Aided by subsidies from the Department of the Secretary of State and other federal and provincial agencies, singers, musicians, choruses, theater groups, dance troupes, and other artists perform in French for the students, and for those parents who can be present during school hours to attend such events. Several parents said that these were the only times they saw performances of this nature; this is explained in part by their convenient accessibility and in part by the infrequency with which some of the performers give public presentations.

Still another way in which children enrich the francophone life-style of their parents is through participation in their own staged activities at school. It is rare for most parents, whatever their linguistic background, to miss their child's involvement in the class play, the Christmas program, or the spring field day. True, such events typically happen only once a year; hence their effect on the life-style of the parents is only significant when considered cumulatively. However, the multigame schedule of league-based sports teams in the upper grades has a more direct effect. Preparation for a given event and discussion both before and afterward also constitute a significant part of the francophone parent's life-style. Finally, the child's staged activities and the surrounding discussion in French add a special dimension to the linguistic bond that unites the child and his or her parents.

Extracurricular Activities

The Achilles' heel of francophone survival in Calgary is the dearth of extracurricular activities in French for its youth. What is worse is that the number of activities of this kind seems to decline as those who would participate in them grow older and, ironically, as the need for them becomes more acute. In other words, as young francophones enter their adolescent years, they, like so many other Canadians of the same age, become increasingly sensitive to the interests and expectations of their peers, including those whose mother tongue is English. At a time in life when they are most inclined to conform to the ways of their friends and acquaintances, they are, largely because they have very little choice, most likely to be in contact with anglophones and anglophone youth culture.

It is not that francophone parents and community leaders are unaware of, or unconcerned about this situation. Much to the contrary, they worry about it a great deal, principally because they feel so powerless to combat it. Teen-age activities are generally more expensive than children's activities and often require larger numbers of participants to make them possible. A child might take lessons on the violin for several years, playing alone to a point where his or her teacher recommends some ensemble experience.

Often the best place to find that is in the city's youth orchestra, most members of which, however, are anglophone. The parent who would like to encourage a child who loves music to continue to develop his or her skills is now faced with an ugly choice between cherished goals: the goals of the francophonie on the one hand, or the goal of the child's artistic development, on the other. Or consider the child who can be thrilled with a trip to the zoo or to the planetarium, events costing relatively little. As an adolescent who has already done these things, he or she now wants to play on a hockey or basketball team or start taking drama classes. Some of these activities are more expensive than others, but all require a certain minimum number of participants.

The francophone parents' concern is grounded in the observation that their offspring have considerable time available each day and throughout the year when school is not in session and family activities are unavailable. With anglophone children living in the neighbourhood, the possibility of sampling the wares of the dominant culture is everpresent and tempting. The temptation and the opportunity to sample increase as the French-speaking child grows older, moves into adolescence, acquires more and more independence, and develops specialized tastes. Appealing francophone extracurricular activities could go a long way toward counteracting the pull of the anglophone world were they available in sufficient number and variety.

There exists for the francophone children of the city a handful of organized activities and specialized clubs with their own programs of activities which are operated more or less independently of the family and the school. Both the Boy Scouts of Canada and the Girl Guides of Canada have maintained francophone chapters in Calgary since 1986. Les scouts and les guides are affiliated with Église Sainte-Famille. In addition, a springtime children's theater festival now features one or two plays in French. On a more informal level, the church organizes several different activities for children and adolescents, some of which are regular, some of which are one-time-only affairs.

In the summer, francophone and francophile children ages six to twelve can attend one or more weeks of artistic, athletic, and outdoor activities at the Terre des Jeunes camp. The camp, founded in 1975 under another name, is financed by, among others, Roynat, individual donations, and La Banque Nationale du Canada (Bertrand 1992: 1). Because francophone parents have the same worries about camp as they do about school, a special group strictly for francophone children is formed each year when enrolments are sufficient.

Calgary also has its own chapter of the Francophonie Jeunesse de l'Alberta (FJA), known as the Voyageurs de Calgary. The FJA was founded in 1972 by and for the province's French-speaking youth between the ages of fourteen and twenty-five. Members of the Voyageurs take part in, or work on local and provincial activities and projects designed to promote French-Canadian culture and develop young Franco-Albertan talent in the fields of sport, culture, business, leisure, politics, education, communications, and public affairs. The FJA stresses that participation in its activities and projects should be both constructive and enjoyable, participation that can be classified in many instances as serious leisure (see chapter 5).

To foster the growth of business acumen, the FJA has established the Compagnie Jeunesse de Services whose raison d'être is to provide members with experience in management, leadership, public relations, and the democratic process. The services offered by the young people include day care, lawn mowing, office work, housework, and residential or commercial maintenance. In addition, some of its athletes participate in the annual Jeux Olympiques francophones de l'Alberta, which were held in 1993 for the second straight year. The Voyageurs is the only organization in Calgary devoted exclusively to the needs of the city's French-speaking adolescents and young adults.

Apart from these activities and those associated with the school, such as the sports contests, arts projects, the annual science fairs, and bilingual debates, little else is available on the formal level for the francophone youth of Calgary. Nevertheless, some do find their way into interest groups composed of both late-adolescent and young and even middle-aged adults. Those who participate in francophone improvisational theatre exemplify this form of participation, as do those who participate in certain sports (see chapter 5).

About the informal level of teen-aged activities I can only speculate, since the matter was never systematically explored in the interviews. Still, it seems likely that children and adolescents attending École Sainte-Anne would develop friendships with their classmates, leading them to spontaneously arrange activities and get-togethers on weekends, after school hours, and during holiday periods. How much French is spoken during these gatherings and how much contact there is with francophone culture are two unanswered questions of great importance. In principle, such friendships, were they based on a strong commitment to French and francophone culture, could go a long way toward reinforcing the efforts teachers and parents are making to reach the four goals. Reinforcement could take place even though the child or adolescent also associates with neighborhood anglophones during some of the hours away from school, as the interviews suggest they do.

Parents can play a key role in promoting francophone friendships. They must be willing to provide transportation so their children can play with francophones living in other parts of the city. They must also be willing to nurture these relationships, for instance, by encouraging their own son or daughter to invite friends to stay overnight at their home, attend a birthday party there, or join the family in an outing of some kind. Finally, they must be willing to direct their children and their friends toward francophone events or toward events that, although linguistically neutral, still stimulate talk (in French). Many informal activities are both linguistically neutral and appropriate for small groups of children and adolescents, including skating, skiing, hiking, tobogganing, flying kites, and other sports. Certain amateur activities in the arts and sciences with appeal to adolescents can also be linguistically neutral, and therefore good places to generate discourse in French (astronomy, mineralogy, photography, amateur music, and improvisational theatre). Some hobbies (canoeing, fishing, nature study, and playing computer games) can serve the same purpose.

It may be that at least some parents are meeting this challenge.

Hébert (1993) reported in her study of friendship patterns among francophone students in Grades seven and eight at École Sainte-Anne that the girls' closest friends were either bilingual or francophone. The boys were more adventuresome, however; they had moved farther into the wider community. Accordingly, their closest friends were either bilingual or anglophone.

Further analysis of the interviews indicates that through their emotional bond, parents can foster a positive emotional association between their children and the French language and its cultures (Stebbins 1992c). The social-psychological process of cognitive consistency underlying this generalization operates as follows: if two people love and respect each other, they are both likely to love and respect a third object cherished by one of them (Berscheid 1985: 426–8). Viewed from another angle, shared sentiments bringing parents and children closer together in this way are likely to stimulate the children to emulate their parents still more – that is to say, to be more francophone. Love is an important component in this emotional bonding, as is respect for the child and his or her accomplishments in life. A third component is encouragement, although certainly not excessive pressure, to do well at what he or she sets out to do, including learning French and undertaking activities in French. A number of Calgary francophones and franco-philes have learned that at home, at school, and in the domain of extracurricular activities, these three sentiments can do wonders to promote loyalty to the French community on all levels – local, national, and international.

Conclusion

It is hardly surprising that francophones in Alberta and elsewhere in Canada outside Quebec fight so tenaciously to secure the right to educate their children in French. The school is one of the two main centers of francophone activity for these children. It joins the family, especially the type of family that develops around the endogamous marriage, as one of the two main avenues leading to the realization of the goals of maintenance and transmission of the French language, as well as personal and community development.

In terms of importance, childrens' and adolescents' extracurricular activities rank a distant second behind these two institutions.

Yet if they were more extensive and better developed, extracurricular activities could in principle play as strong a role in helping francophones reach the four goals as the family and the school do. But attending to their development is one of the greatest challenges facing the adult members of the urban francophonie. Federal subsidies, noticeably reduced in recent years by budget cuts, are available for formal activities and for clubs and associations willing to organize them. The weakened programs of the Secretary of State are not, however, the only forces behind the underdevelopment of formal extracurricular activities. The sheer reality of small numbers must be reckoned with as well. More importantly, however well developed the formal activities in the francophone community, it is the informal side of the extracurricular world that will provide most of the fertile soil needed for the growth of francophone solidarity among children and adolescents. In other words, these young Franco-Calgarians may be more attracted to, and consequently be more prepared to spend time in, the spontaneous and informal side than in the organized and formal side of their community.

Looming on the horizon is the intractable problem of the relève: will there be a future generation of francophones to replace the present generation of adults in such places as Calgary? Somehow, children and youth must be encouraged to retain their francophone heritage, especially their language, even as they are learning English and enjoying a certain amount of anglophone culture. Many of the activities and energies of adult francophones in Calgary are directed toward ensuring the relève. Without those activities it is questionable whether young Franco-Calgarians would retain for long their commitment to their distinctive ethnic background.

5

Adult Linguistic Life-styles

Calgarians who speak French, are married, and have a family can lead a second francophone life-style that unfolds more or less independently of the needs and interests of their children. This *adult* life-style varies considerably according to whether the francophone or francophile is part of an endogamous or exogamous marriage. Furthermore it is substantially different from the adult life-style led by those free in one way or another of children and who, it should be noted, constituted the majority of the sample. Fifty-three respondents were childless, single, divorced, widowed, or living as couples whose children had grown up and left home. Thus both the type of marriage and the presence or absence of children affect the amount and rate of participation in the adult sector of the francophonie.

For the most part, adult francophone activities in Calgary must be appealing enough to compete with the plethora of attractions constantly beckoning from the anglophone sector. This condition holds because most Franco-Calgarians are bilingual, because their participation in the Calgary French community is largely voluntary, and because they, like other people, are disinclined to volunteer to do something unless they can profit in some way from it. Since few practical, or extrinsic gains can be realized from such participation, we are forced to conclude that it is motivated by intrinsic gain, by its potential for interest, enjoyment, fulfilment, self-actualization, and similar benefits.

It appears that the francophone activities pursued by adults in Calgary meet the condition of attractiveness rather well, for this study clearly demonstrates that the adult francophone life-style in the city is built chiefly on the pursuit of leisure in French. The respondents spoke in diverse ways about the interest, enjoyment, fulfilment, and self-actualization they gained from voluntarily participating in French in the different adult activities available to them. The meaning of these activities for them is consistent with the standard subjective definition of leisure developed by sociologists. Since it turns out that activities defined as leisure are also found in the spheres of school, work, family, volunteering, and organizational life, the subject of leisure will reappear frequently throughout the remainder of this book.

The Leisure Perspective

Kelly (1990: 7) defines leisure as 'an activity chosen in relative freedom for its qualities of satisfaction.' According to Kaplan (1960: 22–5) leisure can be further distinguished from other kinds of human activity by seven essential elements. He theorized that leisure is or involves:

1. an antithesis to 'work' as an economic function;
2. a pleasant expectation and recollection;
3. a minimum of involuntary social-role obligations;
4. a psychological perception of freedom;
5. a close relation to the values of the culture;
6. an inclusion of an entire range [of activities] from inconsequence and insignificance to weightiness and importance;
7. often, but not necessarily, an activity characterized by the element of play.

This definition with its seven elements suggests that leisure is sought first and foremost for intrinsic reasons, as an end in itself, rather than for extrinsic reasons, as a means to an end.

This conceptualization of leisure is logically consistent with the more subjective approach set out in chapter 1, namely, that leisure activities are activities defined as such by those engaging in them (see Shaw 1985, for a discussion of the empirical basis of this approach). As indicated, it is the activities carried out in French and defined by francophones and francophiles as leisure that are of interest in this study. For example, certain activities exist for adults and children which are, understandably, more likely to be attractive to, more likely to be seen as leisure by, parents whose children are living at home than parents whose children have 'left the nest.'

One of the many ways to classify leisure is by the degree of seriousness with which it is regarded by those who pursue it (Stebbins 1992b: chapter 1). 'Serious leisure' is the systematic pursuit of an amateur, hobbyist, or volunteer activity sufficiently substantial and interesting in nature for the participant to find a career there in the acquisition and expression of a combination of its special skills, knowledge, and experience. It is usually contrasted with 'casual' or 'unserious' leisure, which is considerably less substantial and offers no career of the sort just described. Casual leisure can also be defined residually as all leisure falling outside the three main types of serious leisure.

The three types of serious leisure are amateurism, hobbyist activities, and career volunteering. Amateurs are found in the art, science, sport, and entertainment fields, where they are inevitably linked in one way or another with professional counterparts who coalesce, along with the public whom the two groups share, into a three-way system of relations and relationships. Professionals are identified and defined according to sociological theory, a significantly more exact procedure than the commonsense approach (Stebbins 1992b: Chap. 2).

Hobbyists lack this professional alter ego, although they sometimes attract commercial equivalents as well as small publics who take an interest in what they do. Hobbyists can be classified according to five categories: (1) collectors, (2) makers and tinkerers, (3) activity participants (in noncompetitive, rule-based, pursuits), (4) players of sports and games (where no professional counterparts exist), and (5) liberal-arts enthusiasts. Fishing (Bryan 1977), bird-watching (Kellert 1985), and barbershop singing (Stebbins 1993a) exemplify the third category, whereas field hockey (Bishop and Hoggett 1986), long-distance running (Yair 1990), and competitive swimming (Hastings, Kurth, et al. 1989) exemplify the fourth. The fifth category embraces the inveterate readers of works of science, history, specific literary genres, or similar objects of study, who read purely for intrinsic reasons, for the pleasure of acquiring a broad but still focused knowledge and understanding of a major area of human life (Stebbins in press).

'Volunteering' refers to voluntary individual or group action devoted to helping oneself or others or both. It is not done primarily for monetary or material gain, nor is it obligatory (Van Til 1988: 5–9; Fischer and Schaffer 1993: 13–14). When viewed from the taxonomy prepared by Statistics Canada (1980), it is evident that the scope of career volunteering is wide-ranging. It includes seven types of organizations, within which different services are provided: health (physical and nonphysical health care for all ages), educational (service inside and outside the formal school system), social/welfare (child care, family counselling, correctional services), leisure (service in athletic and nonathletic associations), religious (service in religious organizations), civic/community action (advocacy, service in professional and labour organizations), and political (service in political organizations). Although much of career volunteering appears to be connected in one way or another with an organization of some sort, what Fischer and Schaffer (1993: 14) call 'formal volunteering,' the scope of this leisure is possibly even broader, perhaps including the kinds of helping the devoted do for social movements or for neighbours and family, behavior known as 'informal volunteering.'[1] Still, the definition of serious leisure focuses on volunteering in which the participant can find a career, in which there is continuous and substantial helping, rather than one-time donations of money, organs, services, and the like. The case for considering volunteering as a form of leisure was made several years ago by Karla Henderson (1981), who stresses that it has, among its other qualities, the perception of being different from *obligated* nonwork (see also Fischer and Schaffer 1993: 9–10, 107–8; Chambré 1987).

Serious leisure is further defined by six distinctive qualities (Stebbins 1992b: 6–8), qualities found among amateurs, hobbyists, and volunteers alike. One is the occasional need to *persevere*, such as in confronting danger (Fine 1988: 181) or managing stage fright (Stebbins 1981) or embarrassment (Floro 1978: 198). Yet it is clear that the positive feelings about the activity derive to some extent from sticking with it through thick and thin, from conquering adversity. A second quality is, as already indicated, that of finding a *career* in the endeavour, shaped as it is by its own special contingencies, turning points, and stages of achievement or involvement.

Careers in serious leisure commonly rest on a third quality: significant personal *effort* that proceeds from specially acquired knowledge, training, or skill, and, indeed, all three at times. Examples of these acquisitions include such characteristics as showmanship, athletic prowess, scientific knowledge, and long experience in a role. Fourth, eight *durable benefits* of serious leisure have so far been identified, mostly from research on amateurs: self-actualization, self-enrichment, self-expression, regeneration or renewal of self, feelings of accomplishment, enhancement of self-image, social interaction and belongingness, and lasting physical products of the activity (a painting, scientific paper, piece of furniture). A further benefit – self-gratification or pure fun, which is considerably more evanescent than the preceding eight – is the only one shared with casual leisure.

A fifth quality of serious leisure is the *unique ethos* that grows up around most expressions of it. A central component of this ethos is the special social world within which participants there realize their interests. David Unruh (1980: 277) defines the social world as 'amorphous, diffuse constellations of actors, organizations, events, and practices which have coalesced into spheres of interest and involvement for participants [and in which] it is likely that a powerful centralized authority structure does not exist.' Another key component of the ethos of any particular pursuit is its subculture, which interrelates the 'diffuse and amorphous constellations' by means of such elements as special norms, values, beliefs, moral principles, and performance standards.

The sixth quality revolves around the preceding five: participants in serious leisure tend to *identify* strongly with their chosen pursuits. In contrast, casual leisure, although hardly humiliating or despicable, is nonetheless too fleeting, mundane, and commonplace for most people to find a distinctive identity within it. I should imagine that this was the quality Cicero had in mind when he coined his famous slogan: *Otium cum dignitate,* or 'leisure with dignity.'

It is appropriate to end this theoretical exposition with a cautionary note about the obligations that also abound in domestic life (not to mention working life), obligations that can be disagreeable and therefore quite understandably defined as anything but leisure. Some of these, such as transporting children across town to French school, badgering them to do their homework, and monitoring their use of English around the house, are also part of the linguistic life-style of a number of Franco-Calgarians. Life is not easy for people who decide to swim against the linguistic stream. In certain ways, because they have chosen to pursue the four goals of their community, their existence is now more difficult than if they had rejected those goals. Still, in other ways, their existence is also more pleasant, and certainly more enriched, precisely because they have made this choice. Every parent in this study said in one way or another that for him or her the pleasure outweighed the difficulty.

Casual Leisure

Although at present we have only impressionistic evidence to support the claim, it is nonetheless believed that many more people pursue casual leisure than pursue serious leisure (Stebbins 1992b: 135). At any rate, the leisure interests of Franco-Calgarians were consistent with this pattern. In addition to their relations with their children, they maintained and furthered their own capacity in French by engaging in one or more of six types of casual leisure. All six require a reading, a speaking, or a listening knowledge of French. Primarily physical and nonverbal leisure activities done alone, such as exercising, or working on a craft or skill, are given little attention here. Of the six activities considered, four can be, and often are, done alone, but they are nonetheless verbal. These first four are, in Orthner's (1975) words, either 'individual' leisure – leisure done alone – or 'parallel' leisure – leisure done in the presence of someone else but requiring little interaction with that person.

Noninteractive Leisure

For the participants in this survey reading was almost always an individual form of leisure and most commonly of the casual variety. The respondents generally read newspapers, newsletters, magazines, and purchased or borrowed books, with the latter being the most common. *Le Franco*, a long-established provincial weekly published by the ACFA, and *Le Calgaréen*, a new, and at the time of this survey, not-yet secure, independent monthly published for Calgarians, were the most widely read newspapers. Newspapers from Quebec and Europe arrive in Calgary too late to be of much use as channels of news, although some respondents, many of whom are teachers, said that they like to read them from time to time at work for the analyses they provide. The newsletters are typically short and available only to members of the organizations publishing them (e.g., 'Le Bulletin Paroissial' disseminated by Église Sainte-Famille). Magazines were about as popular, in good part because they offer either general news analyses or specific treatments of specialized subjects such as sports or fashion. Books, since they take the longest to cover, can easily occupy the greatest proportion of a person's reading time. Approximately half the respondents spent some of their free time reading in French, most often books, and did so for pleasure and for the maintenance and advancement of their linguistic capacity.

A special kind of reading – sometimes enjoyed as leisure, sometimes disdained as an obligation – is engaged in when cooking from traditional recipes, recipes acquired from one's family or from French-language cookbooks. To the extent francophones regularly prepare dishes or even entire meals from such recipes, they maintain a certain level of contact not only with their mother tongue but also with their ethnic heritage. These culinary specialities can lead to a moderate amount of talk at mealtime about their preparation and their place in the cook's social and cultural background, talk however, that may take place in English in families founded on exogamous marriages.

The second type of casual leisure, (watching plays and viewing French-language films and videos), can be either parallel or individual since it is centered on the stage and screen. Five to six French-language films are shown monthly in Calgary, most of them at the Plaza, a commercial cinema located near the center of the city. In addition, a reasonable variety of French videos is available for rent in certain stores, the public library, and the National Film Board and for purchase from two Quebec-based mail-order firms. Although I never systematically explored the role of the home-made video, it nonetheless appears to augment significantly the audio-visual foundation of francophone leisure in Calgary. For example, some respondents mentioned that relatives living in Quebec or Europe occasionally communicated with them by this medium. About 30 per cent of those interviewed regularly watched French films and videos.

About the same proportion attended the half-dozen or so plays produced each year in French, mostly by the Société de Théâtre de Calgary. A much smaller proportion (eleven respondents) took an interest in the improvisational theatre staged Friday evenings from October through April by the Ligue d'Improvisation. That the latter art is familiar mostly to French-Canadians helps explain this difference in the appeal of the two types of theater. The Voix des Rocheuses, the a cappella chorale, also gives a small number of concerts each season. This study suggests that they are somewhat less popular in the local francophonie than the plays presented by the theatre society. Only six respondents mentioned that they regularly or occasionally attended the concerts of francophone singers or instrumentalists. An even smaller number said that they regularly or occasionally attended the talks given in French on the premises of the Alliance Française or the French Centre at the University of Calgary. These talks occur on average once a month from September through June.

Listening to French-language radio and television constitutes still another type of casual leisure, which may also be individual or parallel. Approximately half the respondents watched French television, although only seven of them did so exclusively. The remainder also watched English-language television, where they typically spent about 70 to 80 per cent of all their viewing time. Consumption of French television often amounts to watching a small number of favourite programs, for instance newscasts, hockey games, talk shows, serial programs, or a combination of these. Members of the sample generally liked what French television they could get in Calgary, but given their facility in English, one or two French channels (depending on where one lives) can hardly compete with the number and variety of English channels available in the city. In late February 1993, several months after the interviewing had been completed, the English community information channel introduced a half-hour program in French called 'Bonjour Calgary.' It contains news about local francophone events, interviews with volunteers, selections from performing artists, and similar features. The program, which is being offered again in the 1993–94 season, is badly needed and therefore could attract a sizeable number of viewers.

Radio held somewhat greater appeal than television for Franco-Calgarians; 57 per cent of the respondents said they listened regularly and exclusively to the sole French station in Calgary, that of la Société Radio-Canada, the French network of the Canadian Broadcasting Corporation. Much of this listening serves as accompaniment to other activities, such as doing chores around the house or driving to a destination in the metropolitan area. Yet hockey broadcasts and particular specialty programs (e.g., 'À la trace d'un maître,' talk shows) were also mentioned, programs where listening is the person's main activity.

Many respondents noted that listening to recordings of their favorite popular singers constituted one of their most cherished forms of casual leisure. Depending on their generation and country of origin, approximately two-thirds of the respondents said they listen to this genre of music whenever and wherever they can, but usually as an individual activity. The automobile equipped with a tape deck is often where this takes place. Anglophone music was not necessarily without its own appeal, but the music from Quebec or France for example is different and directly links the francophone listener with his or her cultural past. Radio and television sometimes offer programs of this kind of music as well.

A number of respondents said they derived a special benefit from these different types of noninteractive leisure activities: reading and listening to French originating in various parts of Canada and the international francophonie familiarize the person with some of the latest words and expressions. Because many Franco-Calgarians speak less French from day to day than they do English, social interaction is a less efficient means than reading for keeping one's vocabulary up to date. Noninteractive leisure, however, does little for the maintenance and development of linguistic fluency; for that one must talk in some way with other people.

Interactive Leisure

Participation in intrinsically, as opposed to extrinsically rewarding, conversations in French is one of two types of interactive casual leisure activity. In both types of conversation, francophones and francophiles can express themselves in their first or second language rather than simply listen to or read about what someone else has to say. As for the conversations, they can be held almost anywhere (at a party, during a meal, on a coffee break, while walking or hiking), and with anyone in the person's network of francophone friends, relatives, and acquaintances. For some Franco-Calgarians the basement of Église Sainte-Famille constitutes a favorite conversational milieu, where many parishioners gather just after mass for coffee and, when served, breakfast. From time to time an organization such as the Alliance Française or the French Centre at the University of Calgary will create a temporary conversational milieu by holding a reception of some kind. The Alliance Française is a cultural and educational organization supported by the French government with local chapters in major cities in 105 countries. Fourteen of these chapters are in Canada. In all these ways sociable conversation is an important means of maintaining culture and language and developing oneself as a competent person in these two spheres.

Some respondents also commented on the privacy they enjoyed in public places when using French; in Calgary one can express oneself freely and openly in that language with little chance the conversation will be understood by strangers. One female respondent observed: 'I speak French wherever I can. It is especially gratifying to be able to do this on the C-Train [Calgary's light rail transit], in a restaurant, or in a cinema, because I don't have to worry about someone listening to us. Also, I am proud to be able to speak the other official language in a part of the country where it is not often heard.'

Hangouts are rare for Calgarians who simply wish to converse with someone in French, and a recent evaluation of ACFA funded by the Secretary of State demonstrates that many Franco-Calgarians deplore this situation (Leroux and Dubé 1993: 9). The University's French Centre serves this purpose well, although it does so almost exclusively for the French-speaking students and faculty on campus.[2] The office of ACFA, which is a place of work, sometimes becomes a hangout for people (nearly all of whom are francophones) who drop in on business and stay to chat on other matters. La Ruelle (founded in 1989) is the city's only French bookstore and quite possibly the only real community-wide hangout presently available to Franco-Calgarians. To some extent hanging out is even institutionalized there on Tuesday mornings when small numbers of people, most of whom are francophile women, assemble over tea and coffee expressly for the purpose of talking in French.[3] Some francophones take part in these sessions too, but they seem more often to come to the store at various times during the day to buy something and to talk for a few minutes with the owners and perhaps other patrons. Some teachers of French courses for adults encourage their students to participate in the Tuesday morning get-togethers or converse with the staff at other times during the day. Its merchandise, its personnel, its reasonably central geographic location, and its Tuesday morning sessions are among the reasons why La Ruelle has become an important part of the local francophonie. Here one can also buy tickets for francophone events; purchase local, provincial, national, and international French periodicals; read announcements about francophone films, talks, plays, meetings, and courses.

For many respondents the largest proportion of their talk in French occurs at home, a proportion that varies inversely, however, with the number of anglophones in the family. Thus it is hardly surprising that approximately two-thirds of the francophone respondents indicated they would like to be more involved with French, particularly socially. Many of these respondents also noted that they lack the time to implement this desire, but that this in no way denies its strength. One male interviewee who was interviewed in English because he felt his French was too weak for the occasion, described his situation: 'I would prefer a much higher level. Yet it is nobody's fault but my own ... To some extent it is a lack of opportunity, but the winters go by so quickly. It's just carelessness. We have the opportunity within our family and [we could] pull in a few friends and make it a night of playing cards once a week or once a month. Its just carelessness. I should belong to [a club].' A francophone woman with three children explained how the lack of time hindered her further involvement in local French circles: 'Certainly I would like a much higher level [of participation]. School is the center of my present involvement, but that is all I do. The children prevent me from participating elsewhere, yet there are francophone activities in Calgary in which I would love to participate. The new school-community center will be good.' The remaining third of the francophone respondents had achieved the level of involvement they wanted. Most of them had married a francophone or a francophile or they worked a substantial proportion of the time in French. A small number of francophones of European origin explained their low but nonetheless acceptable level of participation by stating that Calgary francophones (most of whom were born in Canada) are an uninteresting lot and therefore to be avoided. A couple of respondents were planning to return to Quebec; their involvement was also low, but satisfactory to them.

The second type of interactive casual leisure activity is communication by telephone and written correspondence. Of interest here are the interchanges with friends and relatives living elsewhere in the country or living abroad. Some Franco-Calgarians make phone calls to or receive calls from parents and close relatives once a week. This too is a form of linguistic and cultural maintenance, as is written correspondence. Whether the interchanges are by letter or by telephone, the presence of children seems to encourage more of this kind of communication than when they are absent.

Many respondents reported searching for French greeting cards and announcements to avoid offending friends or relatives with an English equivalent. Those who fail in this quest (such cards are available at La Ruelle and certain card shops) write their own messages on blank cards, translate English cards, or simply design cards of their own. Exogamous marriages appear to generate more of this sort of diplomacy than endogamous marriages, since relatives back home often wonder and worry about the pernicious effects of assimilation in such places as Calgary.

Everyone realized that by living in an anglophone community, they could easily lose a significant measure of their linguistic fluency. Some were uncomfortably aware that this had already happened. Some of the latter were now taking steps to try to regain what they had lost. One male respondent said he 'could see growing deterioration in linguistic capacity. I decided I must become more active in the interest of preserving my own fluency in French. At that point I began to watch more French television, attend some of the plays, and go to more of the francophone events being held in Calgary.' Nearly all the francophones in the study looked on their conversations in French both as an interesting form of leisure occupation and as an important way of maintaining his or her cultural and linguistic identity. In an urban francophone community such as found in Calgary, even certain kinds of casual leisure activities when done in French can be endowed with an uncommonly high degree of seriousness (see Kaplan's seventh element of leisure).

Serious Leisure

Franco-Calgarians have a substantial interest in serious leisure, although it is difficult to say, because of a lack of survey data on the matter, whether this interest is exceptional when compared with that of the general population. Some of their serious leisure is solitary, however, possibly requiring a certain amount of reading in French, but leading to minimal interaction with other people, regardless of their language. We shall look first at the respondents' amateur activities and then at their hobbies. Volunteering is examined in the next chapter.

When asked to discuss their amateur activities, the respondents were most likely to talk about sports, notably golf, hockey, baseball, and basketball. All four are eminently social in their execution, especially when played in spontaneously organized matches. Players talk in French as they organize their games, participate in them, and discuss them afterward in a nearby bar or restaurant. Although a francophone sports league is out of the question in Calgary, bilingual players can talk in French among themselves while playing in an otherwise all-anglophone league. Such a league might be formally organized (university intramural sport) or informally organized (pick-up team matches). For example the 'Flying Frenchmen,' an adult hockey team, play in a league of the latter type where no official records are kept, no playoffs are held, and all teams compete by invitation from other teams.

Aside from sports, a small number of respondents reported enduring interests in the arts, most notably singing, acting (including improvisation), and playing a musical instrument. La Ligue d'Improvisation de Calgary, for example, offers Friday-night performances in improvisational theatre throughout the winter months. Here, 'teams' of adolescent and adult francophones, along with the occasional francophile, present spontaneous collective interpretations of everyday life themes introduced by a 'referee' within the framework of a hockey match.[4] Except when participants are practising on their own, these different artistic activities are nearly always carried out in collaboration with other people and before an audience. Solitary amateur activities, for instance, cooking, painting, and photography, are popular as well. But unless the amateur attends the occasional French workshop or course on the activity, it provides scant linguistic nourishment – with the exception of cooking.

A wide range of hobbies was mentioned. Those encouraging talk in French included bridge, volleyball, softball, as well as family or group skating, skiing, cycling, and swimming. A francophone mountain-climbing club operates out of Calgary. Sewing, gardening, and collecting were the most popular solitary hobbies. One might pursue them using French manuals or French periodicals, but the interactive component is almost always light. A number of conditioning activities can also be classified as hobbies to the extent that they are seen as pleasant and voluntary rather than unpleasant and obligatory. Depending on the participant's definition, then, jogging, rowing, aerobics, and other forms of exercise may be hobbies, although typically solitary ones. Cycling and swimming are sometimes defined in the same way.

Finally, we must examine an aspect of francophone serious leisure in Calgary that appears to have been gaining popularity over the last decade, namely, continuing education consisting of personal interest and work-related courses offered in French. The Alberta Vocational Centre, through its wing the Centre Éducatif Communautaire de Calgary, has been the main source of these courses since 1986. Smaller numbers of advanced language courses are offered by the Alliance Française, Mount Royal College, and the French Centre at the University of Calgary. To the extent that francophones and francophiles take courses in French in, let us say, cooking, sewing, photography, word processing, or advanced writing and do so chiefly for the fun of it all rather than to fill a requirement at work or at home, they are engaging in serious leisure (Stebbins in press). These courses are like lessons in music or skiing; they contain instructions on how better to pursue a certain hobby or amateur activity. But workshops such as those offered for parents several times a year by the Copains de jeux or for specific needs by the Centre Éducatif communautaire are in general most accurately defined as in some significant degree obligatory, although nonetheless quite possibly enjoyable.

Very few of the respondents said they had taken or were taking such personal interest or work-related courses. This may be due to a flaw in the sampling procedure, however, for people are taking them and as a result a few more are offered each year. The courses are a particularly good way to mix interactive and noninteractive leisure at the serious level, as seen in the way the students enrolled in them read on their own, attend lectures, ask questions of the instructor, and mingle with him or her and each other both before and after class. The growing number of francophones and francophiles in Calgary makes such courses realistic; their existence attests to the broad appeal of continuing education for leisure purposes (Kelly 1990: 318–19).

Conclusion

All the activities described in this chapter are in principle available to francophones and francophiles alike, regardless of their sex. In practice, however, the rate of participation in them varies widely according to several conditions. One of these conditions is the type of marriage; respondents in exogamous marriages, especially if they are female, often feel constrained to participate in activities outside the home with their spouses rather than participate in them alone. To the extent that they have these feelings, contact with the French language for these women is restricted to the noninteractive forms of casual and serious leisure they find at home. The presence of children enriches significantly this forced domestic francophone life-style. Several mothers spoke, for example, about how they maintain their linguistic capacity by talking in French with their children. Still, the presence of children may also put an even greater premium on the rare periods of time alone with their husbands, discouraging mothers from leaving their spouses to attend francophone activities away from home.

Francophone women in exogamous marriages also share a problem with francophone women who are single, divorced, or widowed: All of these women find it difficult to participate in many of the activities of the Calgary francophonie, since most of the activities take place at night when many women fear going out alone. Moreover, in activities where people are talking with one another, the lone woman as first-time participant there (and lone man for that matter) soon senses her awkward status as an outsider among people who know each other and want to discuss mutual interests.

A female francophone in her thirties, a recent arrival in Calgary, explained how her mixed marriage impeded her involvement in local French circles: 'I would love to participate more in French events in this city, but it is difficult. I don't like to go out alone at night and I feel out of place at events where everyone knows each other, but I know no one. I could go to films and plays where this makes no difference and sometimes I do that, but then I feel guilty for leaving my husband at home alone. In any case I find that these are not very good occasions for meeting other francophones.'

As we shall see, certain events are bilingual, intentionally providing to provide occasions where both members of the mixed couples attending them can feel at home. My observations indicate that a handful of unilingual anglophone wives and more rarely husbands do come to such events; many of them know each other and therefore tend to talk among themselves for the duration of the evening. The interviews further suggest that many non-francophone spouses, especially husbands, are reluctant to participate in these events for one or both of two reasons: they feel they will inhibit their partner's desire to speak in French or they will be treated as unwelcome. My understanding of all this, from informal discussions of the matter during the years of observation and from the formal interviews, is that the first reason is valid whereas the second is not. Too many exogamous marriages and similar forms of association with anglophones exist in the Calgary francophonie to permit anything other than brief, sporadic gestures of ill will toward anglophone partners or even anglophones in general at bilingual affairs.

Participation in adult francophone activities in Calgary is further fragmented by ethnicity. That is, the French Canadians are inclined to associate among themselves, as are the French North Africans and the francophone immigrants from France, Lebanon, Vietnam, Mauritius, and other parts of the world. Some of these groups are large enough to organize their own activities and, even though outsiders are usually officially invited, they attend in much smaller numbers than their (estimated) proportion of the Calgary francophone population would suggest, presumably because they

feel ill at ease at such affairs. Thus, although ACFA invites everyone, even anglophones, to its annual party, the *cabane à sucre* (discussed in chapter 7), this distinctly Quebec tradition, according to
my observations, attracts relatively speaking only a few
francophones from other countries. Likewise, a guest lecturer from
France sponsored by the Alliance Française tends mostly to attract
the French immigrants in town, as do school events organized by
the Lycée Louis Pasteur.

It is not that these organizations and others like them try to
exclude francophones of other ethnic origins. Much to the contrary, they usually try to recruit them, for they need all the support
they can find and their leaders often seem genuinely interested in
promoting pan-francophone solidarity at the local level. The main
stumbling block, according to many respondents, is the degree of
differentness of the francophone cultures of Canada, France,
North Africa, and the other countries. Even the French language
itself is by no means the same. A female respondent from France
brought up one facet of the problem when she said: 'J'ai horreur
de l'accent québécois' (I detest the Quebec accent). Apart from
occasional gestures of intolerance for certain linguistic differences,
francophones from different parts of the globe have grown up in
different social and geographical milieux, undergone different life
experiences, acquired different tastes in food, and so on. In the
face of all this difference, language fails to provide enough common ground on which these groups can mingle. One interviewee
pointed out that 'it is a common mistake to think that because we
all speak French we all share the same interests. Sometimes people
of French-language expression come from very different cultures.
That can make it most difficult to talk to one another.' At an
earlier time, when the francophone presence in the Calgary oil
and gas industry was at its peak, occupation constituted one of the
shared experiences capable of uniting the French-speaking people
who worked there. But this presence has now been seriously diluted. And strange as it may seem, many francophiles, to the extent
that they fail to develop a strong attachment to a particular francophone culture, seem to feel more at ease in all of them than the
typical francophone who has been raised in only one of them. One

informant observed that francophone children react in much the same way as francophile adults.

Whatever the rate of leisure participation among the francophones and francophiles of Calgary, one might reasonably ask at this point whether the centrality of French leisure in their lives trivializes in some important way the pursuit of the four goals of the francophonie. Or does it dilute the sense of duty and responsibility felt by committed Franco-Calgarians toward their language and culture? Although I am of the opinion that these questions must be more closely studied in the future, I am also convinced that trivialization and dilution are not at present significant threats. Nor is there reason to believe that they might become threats, since duty and obligation are highly compatible with the three forms of serious leisure (Stebbins 1993b). In the urban francophone communities outside Quebec, duty, obligation, and serious leisure seem to be most densely interwoven in the realm of career volunteering. When someone volunteers the motive of altruism links that person's sense of duty and obligation to the (serious) leisure activity in which he or she is engaging. Furthermore, as Brightbill (1961: 177–8) has observed, the leisure institution in modern society is the institution most capable of engendering creativity and inventiveness, personal qualities Franco-Calgarians need in abundance if they are to survive in the anglophone world around them.

In this chapter and especially this conclusion we have considered both the formal and the informal sides of francophone participation in adult activities. The formal, or organizational side, however, is still more complex than our discussion up to this point would suggest. In the next chapter we enter the organizational world of the Calgary francophone community, where, among others, we meet those who volunteer there. There we can see in more concrete terms how duty, obligation, and serious leisure come together as a powerful force in fostering the francophone goals of maintenance, transmission, individual growth, and community development.

6

The Organizational World

In the first chapter we briefly reviewed the two principal sociological perspectives on Canadian francophone formations outside Quebec, one of which was the social structural approach. Much of the research using this approach has been guided by Breton's (1964) and Vallee's (1971) theoretical statements on the institutional completeness of ethnic communities in general and francophone communities in particular. They argued that for such communities to persist, that is to recruit and integrate members, they must develop a network of community institutions, or organizations, as they have been termed in this book. Moreover, these institutions, or organizations must be both attractive and effective, otherwise members of the ethnic group in question will become increasingly interested in the parallel institutions of the majority.

Daniel Savas (1991), drawing on Breton's ideas, studied the vitality of the community organizations developed and used by francophones in the rural and urban areas of Manitoba. He found that the majority regularly used the traditional organizations of the school, the church, and the local cultural centre, but that use of the nontraditional organizations such the francophone commercial enterprises and the sport and leisure organizations was considerably less. Time spent in the informal domain with family and francophone friends was also minimal. He concluded that if the francophone communities outside Quebec are to survive and grow,

their members must also develop and use regularly their nontraditional organizations and informal groupings.

The situation is noticeably more optimistic in Calgary. The
preceding chapters portray a reasonably vibrant informal sphere
for the francophones and francophiles of the city, although some
of them profit more from it than others. In this chapter we shall
see that some of the nontraditional organizations are widely used,
whereas in conformity with Savas's findings, others are not.

Organizational Participation

Franco-Calgarians participate in their city's mosaic of francophone
organizations in four distinct ways: as members, as volunteers, as
workers, and as clients. In terms of pursuing the four goals, being
members and serving as volunteers were the two most important
ways of participating. It was through these two routes that the
respondents gained their most frequent contact with the
francophone organizations of Calgary.

Use of the term 'organization' in this book has been deliberately
broad; it is applied throughout to all formally organized groups
regardless of size. Thus, formally organized clubs and teams are
just as much organizations as associations and businesses are. As
noted earlier, organizations constitute an important part of the
formal domain of the local francophonie. In this capacity they play
a key role in the organization and communication of shared goals
and values and the organization of experiences and the pursuit of
collective interests. Many are subsidized to some extent by federal,
provincial, municipal, or private sources. Together the organizations complement the informal sphere, fostering activities that
only an organization can make possible (political action, religious
services), while enhancing collective activities that are fundamentally informal (pickup team sports, small-group arts).

Although a certain amount of overlap exists between the four
types of organizational participation, each type offers distinctly
different experiences for Franco-Calgarians. Moreover, the level of
participation is by no means equal; different categories of franco-

phones and francophiles have different degrees of involvement in the four types. Among the Calgary sample the most frequent, although not usually the most profound contact with francophone organizations, comes with being a member.

Belonging

At the time of the interviews twenty-nine francophone organizations were active in Calgary, all of which can be classified as voluntary.[1] The largest of them was and still is the local chapter of ACFA, to which over two-thirds of the respondents belonged. Just over one-third of the francophone portion of the sample were members of Église Sainte-Famille, the organization containing the next largest proportion of respondents. The remaining twenty-seven organizations, being considerably more specialized, also attracted much smaller numbers of respondents.

Using the taxonomy set out by Gordon and Babchuk (1959), we can categorize these organizations according to whether they were formed in the main for *instrumental* reasons or for *expressive* reasons. That is, do they promote and facilitate on the one hand, political change, administrative service, or social and educational development, or on the other hand, group participation in intrinsically appealing activities? The first category is exemplified by the various organizations for women, youth, parents, and immigrants. Administrative units such as the parents' committees and the Planning Committee for the Community-School Centre also fall into this category. The ACFA is the principal group in Calgary concerned with the promotion of the French language and culture. The second category contains organizations for sport, children, adolescents, adult social activities, and the arts. Église Sainte-Famille belongs here, as does the Société de Théâtre de Calgary, which organizes much of local French drama and all of local French radio and television. Club Inter and the Club de l'Amitié de Calgary are possibly the purest examples of expressive organizations; however, the first is a friendship group that assembles monthly over lunch for the pleasure of meeting and talking with other francophones and francophiles; the second is a friendship society for francophones age fifty-five and older. A few groups, among them the Alliance Française, Canards Illimités (Ducks Unlimited), the Chevaliers de Colomb (Knights of Columbus), are both instrumental and expressive in purpose.

It is rare for a Calgary francophone to be a member of more than two francophone organizations. The reason is chiefly one of available time, since membership fees, being partly subsidized by federal programs, are low, usually no more than ten dollars. Excluding such work-related organizations as labor unions and professional associations, the most common practice among the respondents was to be a moderately active member of ACFA (i.e., attend a few of its meetings or functions), but to belong to no other organization or club. Twenty-two per cent of the francophones belonged to no francophone organizations whatsoever, whereas 50 per cent belonged to no anglophone organizations. These figures cannot be interpreted as a rejection of the formal francophone and anglophone institutions in Calgary, however, for 78 per cent of the francophones did belong to at least one francophone voluntary organization. Viewed from another angle, the francophones in the Calgary sample belonged to an average of 1.90 francophone voluntary organizations. This figure is over three-and-one-half times the average of 0.53 memberships found by Grabb and Curtis (1992: 377) for French Canadians in general in all voluntary organizations, French and English, unions excluded. Their study revealed an average of 1.04 memberships among anglophone Canadians.

The forces noted in the preceding chapter that limit participation in adult francophone activities in general are also at work in the organizational side of life in particular. Men, and especially women, in exogamous marriages find it difficult to participate regularly in francophone organizations. Additionally, francophiles join francophone organizations at an average of 0.88 per person, where they take part almost exclusively as rank and filers. Their average number of memberships in anglophone organizations was somewhat higher: 1.13 per person. For the most part the twelve respondents from France took little interest in these organizations, with the notable exception of the Alliance Française. They said that they had little in common with the French Canadians who founded them. My participant-observation suggests that Black, Arabic, and Oriental francophones feel much the same way; at least it is rare to see them at the meetings and functions of Calgary's francophone organizations for adults.

Volunteering

Career volunteering was defined in the preceding chapter as a distinct type of serious leisure activity, largely if not entirely carried out in connection with an organization of some sort. In other words, career volunteering is for the most part formal volunteering. Of the seven types of volunteer organizations, four attracted significant numbers of Franco-Calgarians; these were the educational, religious, leisure, and civic/community organizations. Over 38 per cent of the respondents said they had recently volunteered or were currently volunteering on a regular basis for a francophone cause, a figure that is one-third higher than the national average for all types of volunteering by both official linguistic groups (Ross 1990: 12, Table 2). Many people commented on the need for volunteers in the Calgary French community and the effectiveness of volunteering (*le bénévolat*) as a way of reaching the four goals. One woman with an exceptionally rich background in volunteering said 'volunteering is very important for the Calgary francophonie. We have very little money in our organizations to pay people to do what must be done to keep the organizations functioning and filling the needs they are designed to fill. Moreover volunteering is a way of bringing francophones together in this city. We are so spread out you know. Many people tell me that for them personally their volunteer work is one of the most important activities they do in French.' One reason why volunteering is so effective in carrying people along the route to the four goals is that it is almost always experienced as interactive leisure; it puts francophones in direct, extensive, and enjoyable contact with each other. Twenty-two per cent of the francophone interviewed also volunteered for anglophone organizations, usually for humanitarian causes they considered important.

Helping out at a school was one of the most common ways in which the respondents volunteered. Somewhat over half of those with children in school (they constituted 64 per cent of the overall sample) served from time to time as classroom aids, helpers at sports events and science fairs, or members or officers of the institution's parents' committee. Since educational volunteering has been examined in chapter 4, no further examination of it will be undertaken here, except to note that many parents found this kind of leisure to be especially gratifying inasmuch as they could usually mix with their children and share experiences with them. The leisurelike qualities of such volunteering were evident in the enthusiasm with which the interviewees discussed it.

By religious volunteering I mean volitionally helping with church-related projects. Like other Roman Catholic churches, Église Sainte-Famille has a parish council, a finance committee, and a set of standing and ad hoc committees that make recommendations to, and implement directives from, the council. Volunteers carry out the work of these units, and their complexity exemplifies especially well the seriousness of this form of leisure. At the most general level they are devoted more or less exclusively to serving the parishioners of Église Sainte-Famille, or the broader Christian community, or both. More specifically, the parish council and the several standing and ad hoc committees meet regularly to study and look after aspects of this community and to organize cultural activities there. They also see to the needs and operation of the parish. The Dames de Sainte-Famille organize and conduct the church's financial campaigns. All this is religious volunteering of the serious leisure variety, which is not to be confused with religious volunteering as casual leisure. Offering to help from time to time at a church-sponsored potluck supper or an evening for youth is more accurately classified as casual leisure.

Career volunteering in the leisure field is done for organizations whose mission is to provide pleasurable social and physical experiences. In Calgary these organizations come in many different forms, a number of which revolve around children and adolescents. Some respondents mentioned spending a great deal of time helping the local francophone chapters of the Boy Scouts or Girl

Guides. Some worked at the summer camp, Terre des Jeunes, or helped produce a newsletter or other youth-oriented publication. Still others were members of one or more of the committees established to organize events for the children participating in the Copains de Jeux. A small number of adults regularly gave of their free time to organize the social or charitable activities of such groups as Club Inter, Réseau-Femmes, the Chevaliers de Colomb, and the Club de l'Amitié de Calgary. Réseau-Femmes organizes social, cultural, and athletic events for female Franco-Calgarians. The Société de Théâtre de Calgary employs a variety of volunteers in its radio, television, and theatrical projects.

The ACFA is the largest employer of volunteers in the civic/community category, which contains organizations promoting the local French community and its language, cultures, groups, and activities. In addition to the efforts made by ACFA and its volunteers to try to secure francophone linguistic and educational rights at the different levels of government, it also sponsors a number of special annual events, including the Cabane à sucre, Salon du livre (book exposition), and Festival francophone. These events will be described more fully in the next chapter. Each is sufficiently complex to require a great deal of the time and organizational ability of the volunteers in charge.

The Société Franco-Canadienne de Calgary is also prominent in the civic/community arena. It was founded as a volunteer service organization (see chapter 2) whose present contributions include the provision of scholarships for higher education, support of a range of social and cultural activities, and management of Villa Jean Toupin (a residence for the elderly) and of a francophone camping site near the city (le Parc Beauchemin). The aforementioned Planning Committee for the School-Community Centre offers still another outlet for Franco-Calgarians to volunteer at the community level. Finally, the Calgary chapter of the Francophone Multicultural Association of Alberta (l'Association Multiculturelle francophone de l'Alberta) has just been formed to welcome French-speaking immigrants to the city and to aid their adjustment to their new surroundings by familiarizing them with the local francophonie. This group operates entirely with volunteers.

It is sometimes difficult in all this to separate self-interest from altruism; these were said earlier to be the two principal motives for volunteering. Volunteering is an intrinsically rewarding way for people to develop and express their own abilities as well as to experience the good feeling they get from helping others. At the same time, people altruistically help other individuals or the entire community and in some instances both (e.g., by evaluating candidates for scholarships to study in French at a university). Perhaps in an ethnic social world such as the Calgary French community the two motives are especially difficult to disentangle, for anything francophone that benefits its members and commits them to their community also brings the entire collectivity closer to the realization of the four goals. It should also be noted that a small percentage of those who 'volunteer,' do so because they feel obligated to participate as part of their work or part of their preparation for it, and are thus not really volunteers at all (Stebbins 1992: 15). For instance, some of the students who perform volunteer work in the fields in which they hope eventually to be paid to work see their volunteerism as an obligatory means to the second.

In harmony with national data gathered by Ross (1990: 12, Table 2), women in the present study were found to be somewhat more active as volunteers than men, especially when it came to educational volunteering. Perhaps the rate of volunteering will increase for both sexes if ACFA succeeds with its newly formed Banque de Bénévoles (Volunteer bank), the aim of which is to assemble a list of people who, according to their interests and availability, would enjoy working without pay for one or more of the local francophone organizations. Although the interviews suggest that francophiles volunteer at about the same rate as francophones, the observations suggest that francophones devote more time to volunteering. It may be that the francophones, by virtue of their linguistic and cultural background, feel themselves more strongly pulled to this sort of serious leisure than the francophiles do. This difference calls for closer study than was possible in the present exploration. Whatever the truth of the matter, it is certainly rare for a francophile to occupy any kind of leadership position in the volunteer sector of the Calgary French community. Still, the francophile rank and file can help fill the ever-present need for volunteers, while adding numerically and financially to its organizational base.

Work

Translation and education are the two occupations in Calgary employing the largest number of francophones and francophiles who work in French. Even here the use of French is often more limited than might be expected. Translators work mostly alone, studying their dictionaries and the documents to be translated; oral interchanges in French constitute but a small part of their working day.[2] Teachers interact routinely in French with their students, and in some of the immersion schools and all of the French schools they usually talk in French with colleagues at meetings and in the staff room. Immersion teachers almost always meet with parents in English, since as we have seen, nearly all endogamous and exogamous couples send their children to the French schools. But interaction with young children in any language is limited. Moreover, classroom lectures and discussions tend to be confined to the subject matter of the course; general talk is usually only possible in the staff room where, however, teachers pass only a small proportion of their school day. The same restriction appears to hold for college and university professors who teach in French, even including those who teach in language departments.

Few other jobs in Calgary offer this amount of work in French. Those that do are highly specialized. For example, the staff at La Ruelle, the government civil servants assigned to serve the local francophonie, the paid personnel at ACFA, the curé and his staff at Église Sainte-Famille, and the employees at the Société Radio-Canada who produce and animate its French broadcasts are all able to work in French. The main problem is that even where French-speaking colleagues are available, most francophones lack the technical vocabulary to talk with them in French about their work since they typically conduct it in English. Nevertheless, some employment permits a certain amount of French on an extracurricular basis. That is, the job is conducted in English, but francophones and francophiles sometimes converse with workmates in

French during the coffee break, the Christmas party, or the company picnic. Francophones in the Canadian Forces are especially likely to speak in French on these occasions. Some respondents reported even less use of French than that; all their routine work is conducted in English in a wholly anglophone milieu, where their only opportunity to speak in French comes with the occasional request to write or translate a letter or a bill or talk to someone in Quebec on the telephone. Some of the professionals interviewed for this study noted that, although their work in Calgary is mostly in English (they might serve a francophone client or two), they wind up from time to time sitting on bilingual committees in their professional associations.

Sixty of the francophone respondents worked outside the home; the vast majority of these worked in an organization or worked on contract for one, usually as translators; very few worked as freelancers serving individual clients (e.g., the respondent who runs his own audio-video repair service). Thirty-one used French on the job, with the proportion of French used falling somewhere along a four-point scale of 'some of the time,' 'half the time,' 'much of the time,' and 'all the time.' Rare is the Franco-Calgarian who works exclusively in French day in and day out. Teachers, translators, and the specialized personnel mentioned at the beginning of this section could be said, however, to work much of the time in French. Nineteen use French only in extracurricular circumstances, as described in the preceding paragraph, whereas ten use no French whatsoever at work.

All things considered, work as an activity leading to the realization of the four goals is less important than belonging to a voluntary organization and much less important than working as a volunteer for one. This study suggests that leisure is now a significantly more powerful force than work in promoting and maintaining the various francophone life-styles in Canadian cities outside Quebec, especially those without a geographically identifiable French community.

Services

The services available to Calgarians in French fall into three general categories: those offered by government, those offered by businesses, and those offered by professionals. All the services of the federal government are at least in principle bilingual. Those most frequently used by the respondents deal with human resources, passports, unemployment, citizenship, income tax, and the postal service. Some respondents had also contacted the Canada Pension Plan and the Department of the Secretary of State. According to the directory of services published by ACFA in 1993, Franco-Calgarians have a wide range of French-speaking professionals at their disposal. Chief among them are dentists, lawyers, architects, chiropractors, physicians, psychologists, and accountants, as well as insurance, travel, and real estate agents. Each profession listed here has several practitioners from which to choose. An even greater range of choices is available in the business world, including day-care services, printing, construction, and renovation companies, restaurants, floral services, moving companies, funeral services, financial services, cabinet makers, miscellaneous boutiques, and automobile sales and maintenance. Each type of business has two or more francophone outlets. Afficionados of such French-Canadian dietary staples as cretons (a spread made of pork drippings), tourtière (meat pie), poutine (French fries, curd cheese, and gravy), la tête fromagée (headcheese), and fromage en grains (curd cheese) can stock their larders through Calgary suppliers.[3] Poutine is also served in at least one Calgary restaurant.

Were he or she inclined to do so, a Franco-Calgarian could lead much of his or her service related life in French, but very few of the respondents were interested in this approach. Only a small proportion went regularly to a French-speaking professional and with certain exceptions, these professionals were found by accident rather than by design. Only nine francophone respondents said they intentionally searched for a francophone physician. Two of them suggested that they did so because they wanted to reassure their children linguistically or thought that they understood medical talk better in French than in English. The first observed: 'They are used to French since it is the language we use here at home. I think they would be ill at ease with the doctor were he to speak in a strange language to them, at least when they are this young [from an interview with a francophone mother].' The second explained: 'I don't know the English medical terms very well. Therefore I feel more comfortable going to a francophone doctor. Medicine is difficult enough to understand at times even in your mother tongue [from an interview with a francophone female].' This desire to conduct their affairs in a familiar technical language also led small numbers of respondents to seek francophone lawyers, realtors, and insurance agents.

On the whole, the francophone businesses were patronized less than the francophone professionals, although certain exceptions stood out. French preschools and day care (private and public) are in high demand by parents of both endogamous and exogamous marriages, as are the French bookstore and the French and Belgian chocolateries. As for the handful of French restaurants in the city, approximately 45 per cent of the francophone respondents reported eating there occasionally. Nonetheless, slightly over three-quarters of the francophones interviewed said they preferred restaurants where English is spoken. In general both francophones and francophiles expressed a strong interest in 'ethnic food,' with French cuisine being regarded as but one important type. And, as I have observed before, babysitters who can speak French are always in demand in Calgary, albeit difficult to find, especially when proximity is a condition of their employment.

The overall lack of interest in francophone professional and business services can be traced in part to their inaccessibility. Although some professional services are available in different locations, they are still too scattered to be convenient in a city as far-flung as Calgary. The same holds for the businesses, with the exception of those catering to the critical need of introducing children to the French language and its associated cultures. Perhaps inaccessibility would make little or no difference were it not that nearly all francophones in Calgary are bilingual, or at least bilingual enough to use the anglophone services and be thankful for the time saved in travel around town.

Additionally, it has been suggested from time to time by inside observers in some of the francophone minority communities lying outside Quebec that, in general, their compatriots see themselves as technically inferior to their local WASP counterparts. In its simplest terms the inferiority hypothesis is as follows: unilingual anglophones when compared with unilingual francophones have access to superior training and experience in business, the professions, and the trades. Therefore the former can compete in the workplace more effectively than the latter and are able to offer higher quality services there. This theory might help explain the aforementioned general lack of interest in francophone business and professional services. It is noteworthy, however, that none of the respondents used the inferiority hypothesis to explain his or her failure to use these services. It is possible that this putative sense of inferiority, if it ever was widespread, is now considerably less prevalent and that its intensity is noticeably lower in large cities in comparison with small rural communities.[4]

In any case, like the Franco-Manitobans studied by Savas (1991), many Franco-Calgarians evidently fail to see the patronage of francophone professionals and businesses as an important route to the realization of the four goals of the francophonie. They seem to be saying that the survival and development of the local francophonie and its members will be assured in other ways (through the schools, the organizations, and the worlds of leisure and volunteering). In the meantime these services will survive and even prosper, because they have an adequate anglophone clientele and because the francophones who provide them are themselves bilingual.

By comparison, government services were differently regarded. Twenty-nine per cent of the francophone sample (twenty-one respondents) used the French language services offered by the federal government, sometimes in person, sometimes by telephone. Several reasons were given for this practice. One is to demonstrate to all concerned the need for services in French, even though most of those who would use them in Calgary can communicate in English. This point was raised by one respondent who commented: 'I think the provision of government services in French in Calgary is most fragile. That means we must try to use them as much as possible, to show the government that they are important, indeed welcomed. Otherwise I fear that they will someday be revoked. That would do harm to the francophonie [from an interview with a male immigrant from France].' 'I fill in certain government forms in French to show them that French exists in Calgary too. I also tend to talk to clerks in government offices in French for the same reason. They need to know that this country is bilingual [from an interview with a male francophone].'

Another reason is that, given the small francophone population of the city, it is often more efficient to use these services in French. Some of the interviewees believe that when they talk in French, they spend less time on the telephone or in a line waiting for someone to help them than when they talk in English. A female francophone put it this way: 'Me, I use the government services provided in French to justify the provision of those services. It is necessary to show them [the government] that they [the services] are worth it here in Calgary. I also find that it is faster to use the services in French than in English; there are more people trying to use the latter.'

Third, some respondents pointed out that because they read certain technical material better in French than in English, they fill out their income tax or unemployment insurance forms in the former language. Should they need help during this process it is reasonable to seek it in the same language. Many of the Quebec francophones who have migrated to Calgary over the years in search of work have needed the French services of the Federal government, especially during their early years in the city . Finally, when it comes to government services some of the respondents, being equally capable in both languages, write or speak in the first language they encounter on the form or over the telephone.

Nonetheless, the person who would use any of the government's services in French faces at least two problems. One is fostered by the exogamous marriage where the anglophone partner may also have to read the government forms or documents or speak with a government official. This requirement could arise for instance while inquiring about old age assistance or applying for family passports. Another problem is the quality of the French used by different agents. Some respondents complained that at times accents, grammar, and vocabulary were so bad that they began to wonder if they were really communicating with these people. They also questioned the correctness of the information they received. One francophone woman observed: 'I have difficulty at times with some of the clerks I talk with on the telephone. Some of them have very bad accents. I am not always sure that they understand everything that I tell them. Sometimes I have the impression that they don't know what they are doing. One time the individual could not even find the right words to discuss the problem about which I had called.' From extensive discussions with the respondents about this problem, I was able to develop, approximately a third of the way through the interviews, two generalizations about government services in cities such as Calgary: in those areas of government where officials want money or information from francophone citizens, the former will provide good quality service in French to the latter; in those areas of government where francophone citizens want money or information from the officials, the quality of French provided by the latter will be substantially weaker. Once these generalizations were formulated I presented them to all subsequent respondents, every one of whom unhesitatingly attested their validity.

Conclusion

The size and diversity of the population of large Canadian cities become the basis for an extensive organizational differentiation in the spheres of work, leisure, and the voluntary sector. Federal government services in the two languages add to this complex mosaic. Since the urban organizational mosaic includes a rich array of francophone groups not found in the countryside, rural towns, and small cities, the first should show more vitality than the latter three. This presupposes the existence, however, of a population of francophones and francophiles sufficiently large to exploit the natural urban process of organizational differentiation. This, we said, is a valid assumption for mid-sized and large Canadian cities. Furthermore, French-speaking residents in these cities must seize the opportunity to organize, taking advantage of such federal, provincial, and municipal support as is available for this purpose. The present study shows that this condition is being met in Calgary.

'Taking advantage' means taking the initiative – voluntarily doing something. Indeed this is the only real choice, for no *obligation* exists to develop a francophone way of life in an anglophone community where nearly all French-speaking people are bilingual and capable of functioning more or less as smoothly in English as in French. Accordingly, it has been out of a sense of enjoyment of such activity that Franco-Calgarians have willingly started francophone organizations, selectively joined the ones others have started, and enthusiastically volunteered to help them meet their goals. Their actions in this regard are self-interested; that is, they pursue the pleasurable experience of developing and maintaining their own linguistic and cultural competence. Their actions are also altruistic; this means they transmit their language and culture to others and work toward the development of the local francophonie – both activities pleasurable in their own right.

The contrast in Calgary between the centrality of French in casual and serious leisure in general, and volunteering in particular, and the marginality of French in the work and service sectors strongly suggests that leisure is replacing work and service as a key institution in the French communities of anglophone urban Canada. We have already discussed two main components of the institution of leisure, namely the informal spheres of family and adult activities. To it we may now add a third: nonobligatory, pleasurable, organizational life – as broadly defined at the beginning of this chapter – where the large majority of francophones and francophiles participate, and a sizeable minority of them find serious leisure careers in volunteer work.

Yet the leisure foundation of the francophone formations that have taken root in the large Canadian cities located outside Quebec may be even broader than this. In Calgary, numerous special francophone events are held each year that are both enjoyable and memorable, events which when taken together constitute a fourth component of the linguistic life-styles we have been studying.

7

Special Events

In principle, a person could substantially enrich his or her adult linguistic life-style by attending the many special francophone events held each year in Calgary. Still, so far I have met very few people who even come close to achieving this, suggesting that with respect to the linguistic life-style of the typical Franco-Calgarian, these events are relatively marginal. In any one year the typical Franco-Calgarian attends only a few of the total number of events available – because some of them are unappealing, a few cost too much, and other obligations take precedence. The observations and interviews suggest, nevertheless, that together the special events do constitute another important component of the leisure institution of the urban francophonie and another significant route leading to their four goals. This route is, however, considerably more circuitous than the direct routes leading there from the domains of family, school, and general leisure.

But being marginal is not the same as being insignificant, for the special events are clearly remembered as pleasant, anticipated as enjoyable breaks from routine, and looked on as providing yet another kind of setting in which to interact with French-speaking Calgarians. They constitute in short, a category of leisure in their own right. Like the other categories of leisure examined earlier, special events can be classified as either formal or informal, or more accurately here as public or private. As leisure activities they are distinguishable from other forms of leisure in that they occur once each year and more or less at the same time, are inherently social rather than individualistic, are planned rather than spontaneous, and are more likely to be bilingual than other leisure opportunities. Apart from these common features, the special events in the Calgary French community are remarkable for their diversity.

Private Events

Private special events are the province not of organizations, but of informal groups and similar social units, typically families, social networks, and groups of friends. These events fall into three categories: birthday parties, Christmas and New Year's celebrations, and annual trips to visit relatives, almost always those living somewhere in Canada. Only a handful of the francophones in the study participated annually in all three categories, although the vast majority participated in at least one during a normal year.

Private special events are much less likely to be bilingual than those held in public, and with one exception rarely involve francophiles, not to mention unilingual anglophones. Birthday parties are the exception, especially those held for children. Because these are commonly neighbourhood affairs, and even though the child's friends from French school may also be invited, the francophiles and anglophones often outnumber the francophones. Some parents, hoping to ensure that French will remain reasonably prominent on these occasions, said they insisted that everyone sing 'Happy Birthday' in both languages (translated into Canadian French as 'Bonne Fête'), and sometimes, for those who know the words and the melody, that they sing 'Gens du Pays,' a contemporary Quebec folksong composed by Gilles Vigneault and widely used today throughout French Canada to celebrate birthdays. Apart from this, and a certain amount of bilingual direction from the parent or parents in charge, talk amongst the children was said to occur in English or French depending on their linguistic preference at the moment. Adult birthday celebrations were described as evenings of pleasant conversation with friends and relatives, usually held at home or in a restaurant. As such, they lack the distinctive features of a special annual event; rather they are in essence simply another session of routine informal leisure of the sort described in chapter 5.

The most widely discussed special event among the francophone respondents is the cluster of activities carried out during the time of year known in French Canada as the temps des fêtes, or the period running from 23 December through 6 January. Dupont and Mathieu (1986: 27) describe some of the things that Canadian francophones traditionally did during this period: 'The temps des fêtes was for all, Québécois, Acadians or French-Canadians in the West, an occasion for numerous get-togethers after supper with family and friends. They would occur on successive evenings and people would enjoy playing cards, singing, and even dancing. Then they would partake of a réveillon together (author's translation).' The term *réveillon* refers at once to the dinner held on Christmas Eve or New Year's Eve, and to the overall event itself. It is an old French tradition that has diffused to many parts of the French-speaking Christian world, including French Canada. Christmas réveillons are typically more family and child-centred than those of New Year's, which may be conducted with adult family and friends or with friends alone. The meal for the Christmas réveillon is usually served after midnight mass, at which time the gifts are also opened. The New Year's réveillon is organized in a similar way, except that no gifts are exchanged.[1]

The circumstances of living in Calgary have forced many francophones there to modify in certain ways some of their customary activities associated with the temps des fêtes. For most the only family members in town are those in their own nuclear family, a condition that rules out the grand, memorable, extended-family gatherings many of them experienced as children. A related concern as the evening wears on is how to control sleepy or boisterous children without the aid of the usual number of older children and adolescents formerly available to look after them. Moreover, the anglophone parent in the exogamous marriages inevitably has somewhat different ideas about what to do on Christmas Eve, a conflict that often compels the francophone parent to compromise some of his or her traditions for this time of the year.

Despite such modifications, the holiday season continues to be special for nearly all Christian francophones in Calgary, in good part because it is an opportune time to reaffirm their link with their own cultural past. This reaffirmation occurs in the intimacy of the family circle, sometimes expanded to include close family friends, where in linguistically mixed families French continues to be a prominent language, and in linguistically pure families it is the only language. Here, reaffirmation generally takes place in an environment of extensive leisure, although exceptions to this rule are now beginning to come to light. Bella (1992) recently wrote about the ambivalence many wives and mothers feel toward the activities of the holiday season, buffeted as they are by an often overwhelming list of obligations.

The annual trips to visit francophone relatives are often taken during the Christmas season; one reason for this is to experience Christmas in its traditional and undiluted form. Certain respondents, however, said they make their annual visits at other times of the year, usually because they prefer to see their kin during the summer or around the time of the winter carnival in Quebec City. Some are unable to leave work at Christmas for a length of time sufficient to justify travelling so far.

Public Events

The annual public events of interest to French-speaking Calgarians fall into four groups: shows, competitions, expositions, and celebrations or festivals. The show category includes all staged presentations of the artistic and entertainment genres. Francophones and francophiles visit the expositions to view displays of merchandise, services, or objets d'art. The competitions consist of displays of athletic or artistic excellence evaluated by a jury. Festivals are occasions of celebration marked by special festive community observances, which Kelly (1990: 30) has defined as 'communal play [that] celebrates the meaning of being together – the community, the social order, the culture, and even the universe.'

The adjective 'annual' refers to public events that occur either annually or sporadically and that fall outside the framework of a regular series of events scheduled over several months of the year. Some of the so-called annual events discussed in this section are really one-time-only affairs which, however, are reincarnated the following year in somewhat different form. Their organizers often intend them to be unique as a way of enhancing their appeal. Many of the events sponsored by the Calgary French Connection, a small organization founded by Suzanne Sawyer for the purpose of bridging the city's francophone and anglophone worlds, are of this variety (Caillé 1993: 6). Further, some events, although intended to be annual, may not be offered every year because the complement of volunteers is too small or too weakly organized. Not discussed here are a number of francophone events held for the first time in 1993, such as a music festival and the appearance of a francophone float in the Calgary Stampede Parade, the latter resulting from the collaboration of several organizations. These events may or may not become annual.

As annual events the francophone shows in Calgary had a rather uncertain existence in recent years, if not before. Although several shows are presented each year, the complement of shows in any particular year varies considerably from other years. For example, the highly successful 'Soirée des Variétés' presented in 1991 by the French Centre at the University of Calgary has not been repeated since, owing in part to the enormous cost in volunteer time required to produce and promote it. It consisted of an evening of francophone variety acts followed by a buffet meal, a public occasion widely applauded as one of the most exciting events of its kind in recent memory.[2] Since then smaller variety programs have been staged, once after a dinner in a restaurant and even more recently after a dinner at an Amerindian community centre, where the audience was treated to native and francophone music and dance. The Alliance Française contributed to the 1993 francophone show-life in the city by sponsoring a chamber music ensemble from France. This event and a certain number of others such as the salute to French-Canadian culture put on by the museum Fort Calgary in 1991, are intended to be unique. The Société de Théâtre de Calgary holds an annual awards night (Gala Annuel de la S.T.C.) for those who have participated in local francophone radio, theatre, and television, an event that is open to the French-speaking public.

The competitions are less common than the shows. Most of the athletic competitions are organized for students as part of a school program. As such, they are quite specialized and restricted. Francophone artistic competitions have been rare in Calgary, although this may be changing. The first regional male and female singing contest for popular songs sung in French was held in 1993. That similar singing contests are regularly held in a number of other western Canadian communities suggests they could become an annual event in Calgary. In the meantime, the most impressive artistic competition in Calgary is the set of theatrical 'games' played each year in the improvisation league. This is no annual event; rather it is a regular series culminating in a 'playoff' held in the late winter months. The same may be said for the informally organized summer series of pétanque matches (a lawn bowling game originating in France).

Two expositions have developed into annual events of considerable importance for Franco-Calgarians. Both are now held on the same weekend at the same location under the titles of the 'Salon du Livre' for the book exposition and the 'Éventail' for the exposition of francophone services. The first displays a range of French games, office supplies, and printed and audio-visual material and is dominated by a display of books written for all ages. Each year it attracts large numbers of francophones and francophiles, including many teachers who face considerable difficulty trying to find interesting French material in Alberta for their students. The 'Éventail' is held in a large room filled with booths and tables displaying the services and products of local businesses, voluntary organizations, and government agencies. Together, the two expositions drew over 700 visitors in 1993 (Valade 1993: 16).

ACFA sponsors both events, collaborating in the organization of the book exposition with La Ruelle, the French bookstore. Both events are widely regarded as important social occasions. Here, new acquaintances are made and old ones renewed as visitors drift from display to display. A nearby refreshment stand aids the socializing. The two are quite likely the most effective activities presently available in the Calgary French community for attracting and integrating people who want to become more involved in it. They are open during daylight hours on a weekend, an arrangement attractive to women who fear going out alone at night. At such events it is unnecessary to know anyone, for the central activity is looking at the displays, which many people do alone. Still, here it is socially acceptable and personally safe to talk about the displays with strangers, thereby opening up the possibility of getting acquainted with some of the local francophones and francophiles. In addition, many of the books and services appeal to francophones from non-Canadian cultures. Finally, the tables and booths themselves offer the newcomer a wealth of information about the city's many French-language events, activities, and organizations, at least some of which should appeal to outsiders.

Expositions of much smaller scope are also mounted, sometimes annually, sometimes sporadically. For example, the Club de l'Amitié holds a bazaar each year at which it sells crafts, pastries, and second-hand goods. Its fashion show, however, is presented sporadically. Local francophones also rent several booths to display certain services at Calgary's annual multicultural exposition. Although the smallness of these expositions makes them more intimate than the larger impersonal expositions of books and services, the former still lend themselves to easy, safe, social contact with the local francophonie, always an asset for newcomers.

The title of queen of the francophone festivals in Calgary must go to its cabane à sucre, the big community party that drew just over 600 participants in 1992 and nearly 625 in 1993. Originally, the French-Canadian locution *cabane à sucre* referred to a cabinlike structure erected in the heart of a forest of maple trees for the purpose of making maple syrup and maple sugar. It became customary in Quebec, when the sap of the maples was running and the preparation of sugar and syrup was in full swing, to hold a party in connection with the work being done, a practice that has found a place with numerous modifications in the life-style of urban French Canadians across the county. The urban party, although a far cry from its rural ancestor, is still held in the spring around maple-sugaring time, when mild weather stimulates the sap to flow more vigorously than it does during the winter.

Certain traditional practices have not been abandoned, however, including especially the celebrated confection of maple taffy. This is accomplished by pouring warm maple syrup over snow packed in long troughs. The syrup soon solidifies to a point where, by winding it on a stick, the gourmand can suck and chew the sugary delicacy just created. Children and adults alike line the several metres of troughs, winding maple taffy on sticks and talking casually among themselves.

The annual sugar shacks in Calgary are now community-wide affairs, and their the most popular component is this making and eating of maple taffy. But other attractions are offered as well. Close at hand, adults amuse themselves with a sawing contest, while inside a nearby hall sheltered from the nip of Calgary spring weather, the children are being favoured with numerous variety acts presented by clowns, magicians, musicians, and others. As the sun sets, more adult entertainment is provided, some of which is traditional, such as folk dances and folk music, some of which is not, such as raffles and contemporary popular music. A supper featuring a traditional menu of baked beans, *oreilles de crisse* (long pieces of fried pork), ham and scrambled eggs, both topped with maple syrup, and a dessert of *pouding chômeur* (a pudding) marks the beginning of the evening. Once the dishes are cleared away a band starts playing for dancing and general socializing.

Being a community-wide event does not mean, however, that a large proportion of Calgary's 14,490 francophones attend it. Although it is true that many would-be participants are turned away each year because of lack of space, 600 participants is only 4 per cent of this figure, and some of the 600 people were anglophones and francophiles. Only six, or 11 per cent of the study's overall sample said they had attended one or more cabane à sucre. For the most part, the event appeals only to Canadian francophones and francophiles; it holds little interest for the many francophone immigrants who come to Calgary from countries outside Canada.

The ACFA sponsors the cabane à sucre and another festival which, although less well-known and attended, is still an important annual event. This is the Festival Francophone, a day-long set of activities held around the 24th of June. It begins with a breakfast of crêpes, after which children, adolescents, and adults participate in a variety of games and activities. The evening starts with a ceremony honouring the most active volunteers of the past year, followed by a dance.

Although the Festival Francophone in Calgary takes place at the same time as the Quebec national holiday, the Fête Nationale du Québec, and its attendant celebrations, little of the Calgary festival is either québécois or political. Many Franco-Calgarians come from Quebec and many still have strong family ties there, but they are now making a life for themselves in the West where they go about their daily affairs, which are quite separate from what is happening in Quebec. Furthermore, celebrating the 24th of June is by no means exclusively a Quebec practice. According to Dupont and Mathieu (1986: 44) it was an ancient French custom to sing and dance around the fire in celebration of the summer solstice, a practice known as the 'Feux de la Saint-Jean' (the fires of St John's day) that took place on the day that came to be known in Christian times as Saint-Jean-Baptiste. The Government of Quebec proclaimed Saint-Jean-Baptiste day a Quebec holiday in 1977.[3]

The practice of holding an open house falls under the heading of celebrations, because such events recognize and promote the organization to whose premises the public is invited. The French Centre at the University of Calgary holds an annual open house and ACFA and the Alliance Française hold equivalent events, to which they often give another name such as 'wine and cheese reception.' This too is how one might most accurately classify the Alliance Française's annual 14th of July celebration of the Fête National Française, which commemorates the fall of the Bastille on that day in 1789. Open houses are small in comparison with many of the other celebrations in the community.

Conclusion

Apart from their relative marginality, the special events held in the

Calgary French community are distinguished from the other three components of its leisure institution by being noticeably more bilingual. On the other hand, nearly all the anglophones who participate in the private special events are spouses of francophones, which is nonetheless a significant number since exogamous marriages account for 60 per cent of all the marriages in the sample (eighteen of the thirty couples are exogamous). These anglophones are invariably present during the temps des fêtes, usually present during visits to Quebec, and sometimes present during birthday parties, where they mix with the neighbourhood anglophone children who have been invited. Among the public events, the shows and festivals are the most likely to attract a certain number of anglophones. But since they are not family affairs, fewer anglophone spouses appeared to be inclined to attend. Their absence is at least partially offset, however, by anglophones attending from the wider community. It seems the latter are attracted to a particular show or festival because it is advertised as bilingual (some English will be spoken there) or perhaps because in the case of the sugar shack, they are interested in this well-known element of French-Canadian culture.

These bilingual private and public special events serve as a cultural bridge over which anglophones may walk and thereby enter the Calgary francophonie. But they only penetrate its periphery, for their inability to communicate effectively in French blocks their further movement toward the centre. Yet those who cross the anglophone bridge do learn something about the culture and lifestyle of Calgary's francophones. In this manner they form a kind of empathic link with the anglophone community, a link that will always be somewhat superficial, however, because without speaking its language one ethnic group can learn only a limited amount about another ethnic group.[4]

The anglophone bridge is infrequently used in Calgary when compared with another cultural bridge. That other bridge is the one over which Calgary francophones travel when they enter the anglophone world and Calgary francophiles travel when they enter the francophone world. This second bridge is the bilingual bridge. It is an extremely important and well-travelled bridge in Canadian cities such as Calgary; people who are sufficiently competent in both languages use it to penetrate deeply into the other cultural community, not only locally but sometimes provincially, nationally, and even internationally.

8

Being Bilingual

Crossing the bilingual bridge is, alas, easier said than done. First, learning a second language to the point where one can participate more or less fully in the social life of the other linguistic group is a long journey that relatively few Canadians complete, although many more complete it in English than in French. In addressing the difficulties faced by anglophones trying to learn French, Kathryn Manzer, at the time president of Canadian Parents for French, acknowledged that 'for most children, immersion terminates at the end of Grade 8 ... They're not going to get jobs at age 20 with a 14-year old's vocabulary' (quoted in Joy 1992: 11). Second, it is difficult to know when we have, or someone else has, become bilingual and can now cross the bilingual bridge. The usual Canadian census definition of this linguistic acquisition is whether the respondent says in the census interview that he or she is capable of holding a conversation in the other language. Gilles Grenier (1990: 36) explains the problems raised by such a definition when applied during census taking: 'Respondents must therefore decide for themselves, based on their interpretation of the question, if their level of knowledge warrants an affirmative reply with regard to whether or not they know the language. Little is known about how the levels deemed acceptable for such replies differ or about changes in the levels over time. We can only speculate.' In short, whether a person is bilingual is determined by his or her subjective definition of the matter, and since most people would very much like to be bilingual these days, as Grenier notes and this study confirms, there is a built-in tendency for respondents to overestimate their facility in the other language.

Notwithstanding this background of definitional uncertainty, Statistics Canada has concluded that the proportion of Canadians capable of holding a conversation in both languages has risen from 13.4 per cent in 1971 to 16.1 per cent in 1991 (Cosman 1993: 14–15). The number of bilinguals in Canada increased by approximately 50 per cent during this period. Moreover, in 1991 young Canadians were more likely to be bilingual than older Canadians.

Much of the federal government's concern with bilingualism outside Quebec has centred on its progress among anglophones, which has been slow. Since the sample in this study is overwhelmingly francophone, our concern is mainly with bilingualism in the other direction, namely how well francophones in Calgary can speak English and participate in the anglophone world around them. We shall also consider the effect of this participation on the realization of the four goals of language maintenance and transmission and individual growth and community development.

The Advantages of Bilingualism

Of the eighty-five interviewees, seventy-five, including several francophiles, reported that they enjoyed and valued immensely their bilingual abilities. The remaining ten (all francophones), for several reasons, did not. Four of this group knew rather little English, whereas four others, having been instructed in both languages from childhood, looked on this capacity as a taken-for-granted part of their linguistic heritage – 'pas grand-chose' (no big deal) – as one respondent put it. The remaining two were planning to return to Quebec, in part because they saw their facility in French withering in the anglophone climate of Calgary.

The following letters to the editor written by two Calgary francophone women and translated by the author from the 21

February and 13 March 1992 issues of *Le Franco* illustrate the contrasting sentiments that the issue of bilingualism can evoke among francophones. The first was written in response to an editorial published in the 30 January issue of the same weekly.

Selfish people? The Québécois? No, monsieur, realists.

My husband and I are Québécois. We have lived in Alberta for five years. We came ... to learn English ... [and] we have learned it.

Now we are packing our bags and returning to our home so that our three children can learn French. One must face reality. It is useless to fool oneself about French outside Québec! There is no chance for French to survive outside Québec. Let us be realistic and listen: even your children at the Lycée Pasteur (French from France at $3,500 per year) or at the école Sainte-Anne are doing everything in English as soon as they leave the classroom. It is normal, it is the language of the majority. Even in the halls of the school, the posters are in English ... What about leisure? Our children bring home their friends, we hear them typing on the computer, and even when it is a question of a game in French, they translate everything into English. That is everyday living for them. Our oldest has started to speak French with an accent ...

We have therefore done some thinking and have come to the conclusion that if we want our children to speak French and speak it well, we must return home. Money, materialism is not everything. We will start a new store in Québec.

I have only one suggestion to make to the francophones living outside Québec: Are you truly committed to retaining your language? Then return to a country that you can call your 'home.' Québécois fight against all odds to preserve their language at least in one corner of North America. You will be proud to leave that heritage to your children and grandchildren.

A bilingual country is a Utopia whereas bilingual people are possible. It is useless to chase windmills, be realistic and logical: we have one country!

Return to Québec and bring your knowledge, your energy, your courage ... Together we can make our country. We will never again have to hear 'you damn Frenchman' or 'speak white' or even worse in the future.

I look forward to seeing you in Québec this summer, you the brave, the hard-working, the logical and the less materialist.

Vive le Québec!

Marthe Lachapelle

Calgary, Alberta

I read with interest Madame Lachapelle's letter ... and I would like to share with her our experience with life in the West.

We have raised four children. We are involved in the [provincial] French-Canadian associations in Saskatchewan and Alberta. We have taken part in the francophone parishes in the cities where we have lived. And we now have the pleasure of seeing our grandchildren learn to read and count in French in the immersion courses here in Calgary.

It is true that as soon as they are outside the classroom, everything is done in English. That is why, if we want 'the children to speak French well,' as you said in your letter, one must do so first at home by correcting errors, by enriching vocabulary and by articulating. This is what we have done. We would speak French at home and the children would speak English to their playmates.

When they became adults, they were completely bilingual, without the tenacious French accent of their mother, to the extent that one of them, a graduate of the Military College in Kingston, twice had to pass the federal examination exempting him from the language courses. The examiners were reluctant to accept his perfect grades in both official languages.

I would also like to return to the last paragraph of Madame Lachapelle's letter. During our twenty-five years of life in the West, we have never heard 'speak white.' Nor have we ever accepted the distinction made by certain anglophones between 'Parisian French' and 'Québec French.' Each time we have explained politely, firmly, but with a bit of humor that there is one grammatically correct French language, sometimes spoken with different accents. Moreover this happens in English.

We are Canadians and the names of our two families have appeared since 1642 in the registries of the Basilica of Québec, the date of the founding of Montréal. We are happy to have been able to live in several regions of the country. We have always felt at home throughout Canada, from coast to coast – to be sure, according to your own words – without denying of course, the place of this bilingual country in the North American continent.

Vive le Canada!

Claire C. Lamarre

Calgary

Madame Lamarre's outlook is obviously the one shared by the large majority of the respondents of this study, those sharing Madame Lachapelle's outlook having for the most part left Calgary to live in the more purely francophone areas of the country. And like Madame Lamarre, literally every francophile and francophone in the sample who had children wanted them to grow up to be as perfectly bilingual, and in some instances, even as perfectly trilingual as possible.[1] For those who shared Madame Lamarre's outlook, the acquisition of the two official languages, whether by the children or by the adults themselves, was often viewed in practical terms: it puts them in a better position to travel in a bilingual country, to find work there or, in dual language families, to communicate with both sets of parents and grandparents. Some respondents commented on the greater flexibility to be gained in the selection of French or English sources of news or versions of films and videos.[2]

Many respondents also spoke of the more abstract, philosophical benefits that come from being bilingual. Whichever their mother tongue, these respondents found a valued identity in their capacity to read and converse and for some of them, even to write, in the country's two official languages. To be fluent in those languages was considered at once an achievement and a source of pride that many Canadians would dearly love to have. At least some of those who have not achieved this were thought to be envious of those who have succeeded in this regard. The following excerpts from the interviews demonstrate the intensity of the pride that so often flows from being bilingual:

I am proud of being bilingual. It is most important to me. I think I am very lucky. I like being bilingual and want to retain my fluency in both languages (francophone woman).

Being bilingual is something to be proud of. Moreover, one acquires a second perspective [on life] that those who are unilingual lack (francophone man).

Of course I am proud of it. It is snobbish to be able to speak only one language. And a person misses a lot with only one language, whereas two languages enrich life so much more (francophile woman).

Definitely, I am very proud. I like the liberalism of bilingual people. For me, I think that tolerance grows with having another language (francophone woman).

In contrast, two respondents who grew up learning both languages were often inclined to treat their bilingual capacity rather matter-of-factly. Acquisition of the languages came naturally, as part of normal childhood learning. But for those who learned their second language as adults, this acquisition came as the result of considerable personal effort. Some of the francophone respondents moved to Calgary as adults expressly to learn English and to work in order to sustain themselves while pursuing their dream. The respondents who learned their second language as adults – and they constituted by far the largest proportion of the sample – were enormously proud of what they had striven so hard to accomplish linguistically.

These quotations suggest that, in addition to pride of identity, the respondents reap several other abstract benefits from learning the other official language, benefits that stand out most clearly in the minds of those for whom acquisition of the second language was a struggle. Thus, to be bilingual is to be more tolerant, more liberal, more understanding, and more sophisticated about social life than is characteristic of most unilingual persons. One respondent said that 'being bilingual adds another dimension to life.' Its social and cultural spheres look different after learning the new language to a sufficient level of competence. Some respondents also described the pleasure they experience when speaking either of the two languages, the joy of self-expression that comes with using a complicated acquired skill. Here is evidence that the acquisition and use of a second language can, when acquisition is voluntary and pleasurable, take on the qualities of a liberal arts hobby to become a form of serious leisure (Stebbins, in press).

The Disadvantages of Bilingualism

One of the most celebrated disadvantages of bilingualism, at least from the standpoint of social science, is the possible or real loss of a person's capacity to speak his or her mother tongue, a condition that Lambert (1975: 67–8) called 'subtractive bilingualism.' This term describes the linguistic situation of language minorities who, in the course of learning the language of the majority group, correspondingly lose their ability to speak their own mother tongue. In other words, they begin to make mistakes in grammar, syntax, spelling, vocabulary, pronunciation, and related areas of speech.

Subtractive bilingualism was clearly a problem for approximately 15 per cent of the francophone respondents in this study, although, as noted previously, they tended to cite the lack of time and opportunity to speak French as the principal reasons for this decline rather than their intensive use of English. By contrast, the remaining francophone respondents, who were also the ones who were much more fully integrated in the local francophonie, expressed few such complaints. They said they had little or no difficulty with the quality of their French, because they were using the language regularly, learning new vocabulary, avoiding anglicisms, and so on. Linguistically speaking, their bilingualism is like that of many Canadian francophiles living outside Quebec, an 'additive bilingualism' wherein the second language is learned without significant loss to the mother tongue. The additive form develops as a person learns a second language while participating in the social world of the linguistic majority as a bona fide member of that world. The learner nonetheless values and respects both languages and the respective settings in which they are used. What is noteworthy about the Calgary French community is that it is apparently robust enough to offer a similar environment for those who are sufficiently involved in it. Godbout (1992) reports comparable findings from his study of adult francophones in Edmonton.

In short, subtractive bilingualism makes general bilingualism disadvantageous only for those who are weakly integrated into the local French community. It is moreover a disadvantage that community members can substantially overcome through greater participation there. Still, as we shall see in the final chapter, many parents in particular and Franco-Calgarians in general, do worry about the relève, about their replacement as francophones by the next generation. Will their offspring succumb to subtractive bilingualism, even if most of their forebearers have managed to fend it off? And if their offspring retain their bilingualism in its additive form, will they pass it on to their children?

Another way in which the advantages of bilingualism can be diluted for Calgary's francophones, is by being made the object of hostile remarks and actions from its anglophones. Such experiences are possible because the francophones, with their ability to speak English, frequently find themselves in the company of anglophones. Still, slightly under half the francophone sample had no memory of such antipathy while living in Calgary, whereas the remainder, more in harmony with the experiences of Madame Lachapelle than with those of Madame Lamarre, could only recount one or two recognizable expressions of it. Ten of the francophones recalled an insult or two hurled at them or their children while on the street or in a store. Their French accents were probably what triggered the affront, most commonly a verbal one, such as the comments 'go back to Quebec' and 'learn to speak English' made by an anglophone male to a francophone woman. A few respondents in this group whose cars still bore Quebec license plates reported that their tires had been slashed during the recession of the early-to-mid-1980s when large numbers of Quebecers came west in search of work. Another seven respondents described what could be called 'categorical' insults, such as sardonic observations about Quebec wanting special privileges or receiving special treatment from the federal government, observations made directly to the respondent or to a broader group of listeners of which the respondent was a part.

The francophones in this study were obviously not driven from Calgary by such hostility; it was simply too insignificant to provoke a reaction of that magnitude. Now they tend to make light of it all, while proudly noting how their accent has improved and as a result how they are much less likely to be treated in this manner. Yet a certain wariness persists, as in for example, the uneasiness that was felt in the Calgary francophonie during the tense period of the constitutional debate in 1992, or the reluctance to use French mailing addresses for fear that postal workers might mutilate the letter after seeing such words and abbreviations as 'rue,' 'monsieur,' or 'N.–O.' (the recommended abbreviation in French for northwest).[3]

The third disadvantage of bilingualism is evident in the linguistic jockeying that goes on among mixed couples and their children. Since English dominates in these families, the francophone parent must compromise occasionally. For instance, he or she might prefer a French cookbook, but feel compelled to buy one in English or accept it as a gift because certain anglophone members of the family want to use it too. The same applies to the language of the family computer and to that of the videos rented or purchased for home use. Indeed, the respondents were well aware of the power of computers, given their importance and specialized language, as instruments of assimilation to the anglophone world.

Still another aspect of the third disadvantage springs from the language used in the recorded instructions played over the answering machines employed by mixed-language families. The francophones and francophiles in the family have their French-speaking friends with whom they prefer to communicate in French, and the anglophones wish to speak to their friends in English. The most common solution to this problem is to present the instructions first in one language and then in the other. If they take the call directly they may modify their initial response, knowing nothing of the caller's linguistic preference, by greeting him or her with the

French 'allo.' This sounds enough like the English 'hello' to avoid the confusion that would likely arise when using a more conventional francophone greeting such as 'oui' or 'oui, bonjour.'

Mixed-Language Gatherings

Finally the sticky question arises as to how to handle mixed-language gatherings in which French and English are equally legitimate, such as in certain private parties, informal conversations, and business and professional meetings. Only the first two were explored in the interviews. About 50 per cent of the francophone respondents occasionally or frequently entertain francophone guests in their homes. They also entertain anglophones, and sometimes the two categories are represented at the same party.

At the broadest level, these gatherings are problematic because they are a kind of leisure activity. The francophones and francophiles there want to speak French at least some of the time for the pleasure of doing so and for the desire to maintain if not improve, their fluency. Nevertheless, they can all, with a few exceptions, speak English as well. Meanwhile, the anglophones who are present are seeking their own leisure; they are seeking the enjoyment of sociable conversation and its spontaneous expression of ideas and feelings, an enjoyment that ultimately rests on linguistic competence. Some anglophones may avoid these gatherings because they feel they are spoiling the francophones' fun and because they cannot participate as fully as they would like. Still, several respondents talked about anglophones whom they knew who did enjoy them, notwithstanding their limited participation, who liked the multilingual ambiance, the people, and the subjects discussed there.

My observations suggest that North American rules of etiquette require people to make compromises in mixed-language gatherings, compromises emerging spontaneously however, according to the wishes of the contributors to the conversation. One compromise, which is extremely common in small gatherings of two to six people or so, is to speak almost entirely in English, switching to French only occasionally when one of the francophones is unable to find the word or expression he or she wants in English. Another compromise is to speak for a while in one language and then spontaneously shift to the other. A third is to give a résumé of the conversation in the other language, usually English. Or, people sometimes spontaneously split into linguistically homogeneous subgroups, a process that is only possible however, when the gathering is large. Alas, some respondents spoke of their inclination to avoid the need to make such compromises by holding only linguistically homogeneous parties.

Over the years I have participated in a number of mixed informal conversations, both in Calgary and elsewhere in French Canada. I am convinced that they have a distinctive character, one which should be more closely examined than was possible in this study. One distinctive quality is the sporadic interruption of the stream of conversation that occurs when the francophone and francophile interlocuteurs pause to search for the right word or expression. Mixed informal conversations are also marked by a greater than usual number of inappropriate words and expressions used by both linguistic groups when talking in their second language. Among the questions remaining to be explored are those dealing with how these conversations spontaneously shift from one language to the other, who provides the brief translations, what status criteria force the conversations into English or French, when French can be legitimately used in anglophone company and vice versa.

The use of French among francophone enlisted men in the Canadian Forces provides a good illustration of the influence of status criteria. My respondents in the Canadian Forces pointed out that the francophone men tend to associate with each other on breaks and during their private gatherings held after work hours, sometimes on the base, sometimes off. On these occasions they usually talk among themselves in French, leaving their wives, when they are present, to their own conversations. Since a number of the men have married anglophone women, talk among the wives frequently runs headlong into the usual requirement to make compromises, a requirement the men rarely have to confront.

The fourth question, which concerns the legitimacy of French in conversations, may hinge on, among other factors, whether the situation in which it is used is regarded by those involved as one of leisure, where spontaneous choice is customary. The staff rooms at the immersion schools offer a good laboratory for the study of this matter. Some of the respondents who taught in these schools reported that both French and English conversations routinely take place in their staff rooms and that both are looked on as normal behaviour there. Other immersion teachers however, reported pressure to speak only English in the staff room. A few years ago, a similar English-only ukase was handed down at The Banff Centre, banning the use of French among its employees during coffee breaks (Dawson 1991: A1). It appears that the question of the legitimacy of French in places such as staff rooms and coffee lounges rests on the subtle definition of whether these rooms exist for purposes of leisure or for purposes of (predominantly anglophone) work.

Conclusion

It is clear that Franco-Calgarians cross the bilingual bridge only at certain points in their everyday lives. Typically, they do so when going to work, going shopping, and engaging in leisure activities in English. Franco-Calgarians married to English-speaking spouses have even further contact with the anglophone world at home. Elsewhere, the typical francophone Calgarian, but not the francophile Calgarian, remains on the French side of the bilingual bridge when associating with his or her children, engaging in leisure activities in French (including francophone volunteer 'work'), dealing with the French or immersion schools, and for some, participating in church-related activities. Francophones in endogamous marriages have a fuller francophone life in these areas, whereas francophiles, unless married to a francophone, have a more diluted one. In sum, bilingualism for the francophones and francophiles in this study is expressed in a segmented way, which, as we have seen, is nonetheless warmly embraced by the large majority of the respondents and seen in no way as a threat to their cultural future and the realization of the four goals.

But these conclusions about the segmented use of French and

the dominance of leisure as one of its main avenues of expression are inconsistent with one of the reigning hypotheses in the sociology of francophone communities outside Quebec: that the future of French there depends on finding employment in that language (Bernard 1991: 23). It is also inconsistent with the pessimistic predictions of the demographers whose figures, they argue, signal eventual and complete linguistic assimilation (e.g., Bernard 1988). But as Heller and Lévy (1991: 39) have observed, the conditions affecting relations between francophones and anglophones outside Quebec have changed a great deal since the execution of the vast majority of demographic studies. In harmony with the results of the present study, they found in their investigation of mixed marriages in Ontario that both the francophone mother and her children can reduce their assimilation to English when they interact as a family. William Irving (1990: 55), although sympathetic with the employment hypothesis, is nevertheless convinced that the French language can flourish in the francophonies located outside Quebec, but only on a segmented basis, only in certain areas of the lives of their members. Thériault (1990: 138–9), after considering the effect of individualization in the modern world, comes to a similar conclusion: 'Individualization is a pivotal process in our modern world and a value held in high esteem by people today. The construction of spaces where French-speaking individuals will be able to live out their linguistic reality together will have to respect this basic tendency.'

Notwithstanding our list of the advantages and disadvantages of bilingualism, its overall appeal for the francophones of Calgary is, in the final analysis, tempered by the values they prize most dearly. Are they more taken with English and anglophone culture or with French and their own francophone culture? If they have internalized the second and hold it in high esteem, as this chapter and indeed much of this book suggests they do, then they can partake of the first with little fear of defecting to it. In this sense francophone Calgarians share significant common ground with their counterparts in Quebec, as is evident in the following extract from an interview with writer Bruno Roy: 'If you accept North American culture as your own, you become doomed to assimilation. But as French-speaking North Americans, we participate in our Americanism wholeheartedly. North American culture is not foreign, nor a threat. Yet we always remain aware of U.S. imperialism. We are not naive' (quoted in Poulin 1992: 23–4). Roy's observations square with the critique Hastings, Clelland, and Danielson (1982: 190) made over ten years ago of Milton Gordon's assimilation model: 'In our view, members of ethnic groups do not see assimilation as necessarily inconsistent with cultural retention; instead they are likely to blend old and new patterns into a new ethnic communality. Such communality is always a form of partial assimilation.'

9

The Future

In chapter 1 the concept of the francophonie was introduced and defined as a community-like ethnic formation without clear geographic locus, centred on the French language and its associated cultures, and based on a modest degree of completeness rooted in a set of organizations and a vast network of interpersonal relationships. The two main types of linguistic life-styles of the local francophones and francophiles (adult and child-centred) unfold within this formation in the different ways examined in this book. Having come this far, having examined these life-styles, it is now obvious that some of their features are more central than others on the road to realizing the four goals of learning, transmission, individual growth, and community development. In other words, one way in which the Calgary francophonie is socially organized is according to the different levels of importance its members assign to the various activities they undertake in their everyday lives.

Levels of Importance

It is possible to develop a rough, preliminary classification of the importance Franco-Calgarians assign to the various activities composing their linguistic life-styles. The activities pursued most frequently are considered *core activities*; they play the most central role in the life-styles enacted in minority circumstances. They contribute most heavily to the realization of the four goals. The following activities make up this category: activities with one's own children (e.g., saying prayers, reading stories, going shopping, going hiking), involvements with the French schools (e.g., being a teacher's aid, joining a parents' committee), routine passive leisure (e.g., engaging in watching television, reading books, listening to the radio), interactive leisure (e.g., engaging in correspondence, routine sociable conversation, club and organizational activities), and serious leisure (participating in hobbies, amateur pursuits, and career volunteering). For the respondents in the study who use French at work a significant amount of the time, their employment can be classified as a core activity.

Semiperipheral activities are judged to be of secondary importance, in good part because they are undertaken considerably more sporadically than the core activities. The semiperipheral activities, all of which involve French, include attending films at the Alliance Française and the sole commercial cinema in the city where such films are shown; holding or attending private parties, perhaps, once a month; going to plays; occasionally (as opposed to routinely) watching television, listening to the radio, or reading books or periodicals; and low-to-moderate attendance at organizational functions. Activities engaged in once or twice a year are seen as even less important, as *peripheral* by comparison. Being a spectator at, or participant in, the different festivals, receptions, expositions and competitions exemplifies this level.

It should be noted with reference to the four francophone goals that Franco-Calgarians never described the peripheral and semiperipheral activities as unimportant, but only as less important than the core activities. Furthermore, they were aware and this study confirms, that the programs of official bilingualism play a substantial role in making possible a significant number of these activities. On the one hand, these programs offer little or no support for many of the pleasurable activities experienced through face-to-face interaction such as parties, conversations, story telling, and spontaneous leisure pursuits. On the other hand, they do aid French education, children's camps, volunteer organizations, radio and television programs, and a variety of festivals, competitions, and expositions.

Couture (1992: 381) believes the subsidy programs in official bilingualism are indispensable: 'In sum, official bilingualism as a source of employment and activities taking place in French, is indispensable for bringing together the francophones. We cannot develop other institutions and francophone cultural zones if the existing institutions are not first reinforced and promoted (author's translation).' Couture stresses the importance of the subsidized formal sector, while ignoring the importance of the informal world and the unsubsidized parts of the formal world. We have no evidence that the modern urban francophonie in Canada would fail without the official programs. Were they suddenly eliminated, the French communities outside Quebec might well survive on the strength of their formal and informal components, components that are in no significant way subsidized or organized by government agencies. Moreover, one point is indisputable: without the spontaneous formal and informal worlds on which to build, the subsidized formal sector would surely fail even if it somehow managed to get started in the first place. The spontaneous, informal world is the foundation of the urban francophonie's operation in minority circumstances.

But perhaps the communities have grown dependent on government subsidies, and in the course of it all have lost their earlier capacity to function without them. In referring to French Canadian communities at a recent federal economic summit, economist Gilles Paquet (*Le Franco* 1993: 9) argued that dependence on the Secretary of State is 'la meilleure façon de vous tuer' (the best way to kill yourselves). The present study suggests the contrary, however; dependence is not fatal, since the informal world would continue were the formal world to shut down for some reason. Still, Paquet's warning does indicate that, given the propensity in government circles these days to trim budgets, these communities may soon have to face the possibility of operating largely on their own once again.[1] It is also true that governments may fund projects and organizations according to a set of priorities substantially different from the set of priorities embraced by part or all of the local francophonie.

Strengthening the Core

It follows from what has just been said that if Franco-Calgarians want to increase their likelihood of reaching the four goals, they should concentrate first on strengthening the core activities and then with their remaining financial and personal resources, concentrate on the semiperipheral activities and after that, on those considered peripheral. But the francophones and francophiles of Calgary, as well as those in the Atlantic region of Canada, hardly need sociological research to tell them that. They are aware of these priorities. And the priorities are nowhere more evident than in the determination of these French Canadians to implement a distinct form of organization believed by many of them to have the capacity to strengthen significantly their activities at all levels. That form of organization is the school-community centre (*centre scolaire communautaire*).

The School-Community Centre

A school-community centre is at once an organization and a building, providing facilities for French primary and secondary education and space for francophone social, cultural, and organizational needs. In addition to the usual facilities for schooling at the two levels, most centres also contain an auditorium, as well as office and meeting space for local clubs and associations. Some house a small library, an art gallery, or a day-care centre. The aim is to create a geographically based social and cultural rallying point for the local francophonie. This type of centre is an Acadian innovation first tried in Fredericton, New Brunswick in 1978, and subsequently copied by several francophone communities in the Maritime Provinces and more recently by the one in Kingston, Ontario (Pitre 1992: 20). After receiving final governmental authorization in November 1993, Calgary is poised to start construction of its own school-community centre, which will be the first establishment of its kind in Western Canada.

This study, and the evaluation conducted by Leroux and Dubé (1993: 13–14) leave no doubt that Franco-Calgarians are most enthusiastic about this project. It should certainly solve a number of practical problems such as the dearth of organizational office and meeting space, the overcrowding of educational facilities, and the lack of space for performing arts groups. In these ways and others the centre could strengthen local core, semiperipheral, and peripheral activities. It could also raise the profile of francophones in the surrounding anglophone milieu. But it remains to be seen whether it becomes a hangout like La Ruelle and the University's French Centre.

Will the existence of such a centre encourage more of Calgary's 14,490 francophones to become more involved in the francophonie than presently? Will those who are now marginally involved increase their involvement? In other words, in comparing the situation before and after the new centre, will fewer francophones cross the bilingual bridge to the anglophone world less often, and will more francophiles cross the same bridge to the francophone world more often? Bertin Couturier (1991: 3) raises similar questions in his report on the centre at Chatham-Newcastle in New Brunswick five years after its founding in 1986. Only 26 per cent of the francophones in the area it serves regularly frequent it. The director was reported as saying that a greater level of participation is certainly possible and unquestionably desirable.

But what is a realistic level of regular use of a school-community centre in a city the size of Chatham-Newcastle (approx. 11,000 population in 1986), located in a predominantly rural region of historically active francophone communities? What is a realistic level of use in Vancouver, Hamilton, or Calgary, much larger cities with no such communities? The answers to questions of this sort rest on many conditions; one important one is the nature and quality of the activities at the centre. Here, larger cities may have an advantage in the greater amount and diversity of serious and casual leisure available in both languages. Another condition, and one very difficult to assess, is the proportion of francophones who, according to a given census, have assimilated to anglophone society, and who are now francophones in name only. It is probably next to impossible to interest them in a local school-community centre, which means they should not be counted among its potential users. Time will tell whether a rate of participation similar to that of the Chatham-Newcastle centre will be observed for the Calgary center.

Another attempt to strengthen the Calgary francophonie, particularly its core, has for most of this century revolved around the province-wide struggle to gain control of French education. This battle was finally won on 10 November 1993, when legislation was passed that lodges control over French educational programs with Alberta's francophones. Henceforth, these programs will be directed by what amounts to francophone school boards or an acceptable equivalent known as conseils scolaires (regional authorities).

This new system of regional authorities is complicated and for the most part lies beyond the scope of this study. Let us simply recall that until November of 1993 the responsibility for such functions as curriculum, administration, and employment of teachers in the French schools lay with the Roman Catholic school boards. These boards were composed chiefly of anglophones, many of whom were either neutral or unsympathetic toward the needs and claims of francophones, attitudes they shared with their predecessors dating back to the days of Rouleauville. ACFA had championed these educational needs and claims for many years, but only recently did the Government of Alberta begin to respond positively to them. The latter has now agreed, in collaboration with the Government of Canada, to set up a system of 'regional authorities' that will operate in every way like school boards, except that they will lack the power to collect taxes. This system will give to all Franco-Albertans a significant measure of control over a core activity in their pursuit of a francophone life-style.

Pessimism, Optimism

These signs of new strength at the core of the Calgary French community contrast with the pessimism I heard from many respondents about the prospects for the relève and, by implication, the prospects for the community itself. Earlier we discussed the decline in the proportion of francophones in Canada, the slow growth in their absolute number, and the equally slow growth in the proportion of bilingual persons. Bernard's (1991) study of Canadian francophone youth living outside Quebec reveals that increasingly they see themselves as bilingual persons first and francophones second. Seventy-five per cent of his sample indicated that French was the language used at home, but only 42 per cent described themselves as being more at ease communicating in French than in English.

Another reason for pessimism is the growing number of mixed marriages. An article on the subject recently published in *Le Chaînon* (1993: 2–3) sketches some of the changes we can expect as a result of this trend. In every province except Quebec many more exogamous marriages are recorded among younger age groups than among older age groups. In some provinces the rate of these marriages among those aged fifteen to twenty-four years surpasses by more than 100 per cent the rate among those aged sixty-five years and older. The article also calls attention to a practice we discussed at length in chapter 3; English tends to dominate in families founded on mixed marriages. As a consequence of all this the article predicts that French schools outside Quebec will serve a growing proportion of bilingual pupils in the years to come.

The present study suggests however, that bilingualism and mixed marriages do not necessarily eventuate in assimilation to English, to crossing more or less permanently the cultural bridge to the anglophone world. Those who value their French language and their francophone culture and who actively participate in the local francophonie will survive their bilingualism as fundamentally francophone people.[2] As this study demonstrates, a most important avenue for such participation for urban francophones (Beaudoin's [1988] *nouveaux francophones*) is through the many casual and serious leisure activities available in the family, school, religious, and leisure spheres of life. Literally all these activities must be generated in one way or another by francophones and francophiles themselves, even though some of the activities will subsequently be supported by official agencies. In the end it will fall to the active, enthusiastic, visionary individuals, groups, and networks to determine the future course of such formations as the Calgary French community. Recognizing the fragility of their situation, they must seize the initiative and create an appealing francophone social environment sufficient to offset the great range of attractions in the anglophone world. To repeat, that environment for most francophones consists of interaction in French at home, at school, at church, and in the clubs and organizations, much of which is essentially a leisure environment.

Furthermore, Franco-Calgarians have available to them an important but as yet largely untapped resource – the sizeable flow of francophone immigrants into the city. Unfortunately this study incorporated very few of those from Asia, Africa, and the Middle East, chiefly because they only rarely participate in the core activities of the francophonie. Yet, as Churchill and Kaprielian-Churchill (1991: 86–7) point out, these are precisely the immigrants who are arriving in the greatest numbers. The authors conclude 'that it is in the best interest of all Franco-Canadians that the human potential represented by Francophone immigrants should be added to the already existing communities in order to strengthen the Canadian *francophonie*.' Although this may well be easier said than done, the newly formed Calgary branch of the Association Multiculturelle Francophone de l'Alberta (AMFA) has as one of its principal goals just this recommendation. One of its challenges will be to find a way to mediate the clash of values that invariably emerges when non-Christian francophone immigrants want to enrol their children in the city's only French schools, which are Roman Catholic. The small number of exceptions granted each year in this regard seem to be insufficient (see chapter 4).

Based on this research, I am led to conclude that a large number of Calgary's francophones and francophiles hold their French language and francophone culture in high regard. I also believe that this is the foundation for what Bocquel (1990: 119) calls the *normalitude* of French and English in their everyday lives. In other words, they sense they are no longer obligated to favour one language over the other. Bocquel goes on to explain that 'it [*normalitude*] is simply having the freedom not to have to choose anymore between French and English, at which point they [francophones] have decided individually to preserve a francophone dimension of their identity' (author's translation). It is entirely natural for the vast majority of Franco-Calgarians to use the two languages in their daily affairs, even while they are especially drawn toward – but not forced into – the use of French because of their strong attachment to it and to an associated culture.

Such an orientation inspires confidence it seems, for no small number of Franco-Calgarians are at present boldly pushing forward with characteristic fervour, albeit a fervour mixed with cautious optimism. That is, no one is overconfident; there will very likely be further reductions in government funding of important programs, setbacks in their efforts to retain control of the schools, and possibly worse (c.f., Le Tourneau 1988: 309). But many believe that the immediate future is theirs, that they can personally arrange for the survival and prosperity of the French language and its various cultures in Calgary. And whereas the distant future holds more uncertainty, they know that the present-day combination of French language, leisure, and linguistic life-style, interwoven with the surrounding anglophone world, will play a vital role in carrying them through.

Appendix:
Interview Guide for the Study of French-Language Life-styles
(*translated*)

With the exception of those in section A, the questions in this guide were developed to explore further several key beliefs, attitudes, and activities associated with French language, leisure, and linguistic life-style in Calgary. I became aware of these considerations and their importance in the course of conducting the participant observation. The questions in section A are of the standard demographic variety commonly posed in sociolinguistic research.

A. Personal Background of Interviewee and Spouse

1. Language: Are you francophone, anglophone, or francophile?
2. Origins: Where were you born? Where were you raised?
3. Schooling: What is your highest level of schooling? What was the last educational institution you attended?
4. What year did you arrive in Calgary?
5. What is your present occupation?

B. Home

1. French: When do you speak French at home (probes: during meals, during television programs, during family reunions, all the time)?
2. English: When do you speak English at home (use probes similar to B1)?

3. What other activities do you do in French (probes: reading [newspapers, magazines, books], watching television, listening to the radio, watching films and videos, listening to recorded music, playing games, etc.)?
4. What other activities do you do in English (use probes similar to B3)?
5. What special francophone practices do you engage in, including meals, holidays (Christmas, Easter, birthdays), St-Jean-Baptiste, Thanksgiving, sending greeting cards, attending the local cabane à sucre?

C. School (primary and secondary)

1. Do you have children? What are their names?
2. Do your children go to a French school, immersion school, English school with French as a second language, English school without French as a second language?
3. Do you participate in school-related activities? What are these activities?

D. Organizations

1. Are you a member of one or more francophone or anglophone clubs or associations, including those that are religious and political? What are the names of these clubs and associations?
2. How regularly do you participate in these clubs and associations, in their meetings, their regular and special activities?

E. Leisure

1. What are your leisure activities (at home and away from home), including (a) films, concerts, plays, sports events, museums, art galleries; (b) hobbies; (c) volunteer activities; (d) eating out; (e) sports and exercise; (f) amateur activities; (g) sociable conversation; (h) reading; (i) adult education courses (j) exhibitions?

2. Which leisure activities do you do primarily in French, in English?

3. As for leisure activities done primarily in French, which do you do with members of your family (nuclear, extended), with your friends, with your workmates? Ask the same question for activities done primarily in English.

F. Work

1. Do you work primarily in French, English, or a combination of the two languages? Describe the circumstances in which you use French, English.

2. Have you or are you taking courses in French or English related to your work?

G. Parties and Other Get-Togethers

1. How often do you get together with others on a social basis and speak French, speak English? Does this happen primarily at home or outside the home?

2. Are some of these get-togethers conducted in both French and English?

H. Professional and Personal Services

1. Which francophone professional and personal services do you use? (available services: physician, dentist, beautician, barber, accounting, auto repair, dry cleaning, butcher, bakery, insurance, optometrist, veterinarian, baking, real estate, day care, Scouts/Guides, government services

I. Trips, Tourism

1. Do you travel from time to time to francophone communities, regions, or countries on business, as a tourist?

2. Do you visit relatives or friends who live in francophone communities, regions, or countries?

J. Interpretation

1. Is the use of French or English problematic at home?

2. While living in Calgary have you or your children experienced discrimination, insults, or ridicule because you (they) speak French?

3. Considering your present level of involvement in francophone activities and practices, would you prefer that it be higher or lower in the future? Or is your present level just right? Explain.

4. Considering your present level of involvement in anglophone activities, would you prefer that it be [at a] higher or lower level in the future? Or is your present level just right? Explain

5. (if bilingual) Do you like your bilingual life-style? Are you proud of your capacity to speak the two languages?

6. Do you hope that your children will grow up to be bilingual?

Notes

Chapter 1

1 Except where noted otherwise the mother-tongue definitions of francophone and anglophone are used throughout this book. As Joy (1992: 23) has pointed out, use of these definitions results in more people being counted as francophone than when francophone is defined more strictly, as someone whose home language is French. But the mother-tongue definition is also the older definition used by Statistics Canada; it therefore affords comparisons farther back in time. The home-language definition has only recently begun to be used and then only in conjunction with the older definition.

2 George Hillary Jr. (1955) analysed ninety-four sociological definitions of community.

3 The census data for Ottawa are presented in combination with Hull, Quebec, as the Ottawa-Hull CMA. I estimated the francophone population of Ottawa by calculating 25 per cent of the overall Ottawa population, the approximate proportion of francophones to anglophones prevailing there for 150 years (Taylor 1988: 1595).

4 Maillardville emerged between 1908 and 1910 as a community of francophone workers recruited from Quebec and Saskatchewan to work in a sawmill on the Fraser River. Villeneuve (1983: 134) reports that the francophonie there began an accelerated decline in

the 1950s, reaching a point today where, according to impressionistic evidence, little activity takes place in French (Bélanger 1992: 4; Société Radio-Canada 1992). Still, such claims about community demise may be premature, given Sylvain Tellier's (1993: 7) report that Maillardville's caisse populaire, the Village Credit Union, has just experienced a major expansion.

5 Relative to the size of the anglophone population, the proportion of francophones in Canada and in its major cities is declining, even though they are increasing in absolute numbers. The absolute number is the more important figure for the study of life-styles, since it more directly confronts the question of the minimum number of people needed to sustain a francophone way of life in an anglophone milieu.

6 Our overall sample consisted of over 4,000 francophones and francophiles living in the Calgary CMA. This sample was composed in part of all members of the francophone organizations in the city. We tried to reach as many of the nonorganized francophones as possible through the snowball procedure and through their children enrolled in the French and immersion schools. Our ideal was to survey every francophone and francophile adult in the community, but the nonorganized part of it turned out to be impossible to contact completely. And, as in all survey research, the return rate for our questionnaires was far from ideal.

7 Although extensive description often by means of narrative accounts from respondents is the fashion these days in field studies (Van Maanen 1988: 49), it impedes effective construction and reporting of grounded theory: 'The most important thing to remember is to *write about concepts, not people* ... Indicators for the concepts which are descriptive statements are used only for illustration and imagery. They support the concept, they are not the story itself. They help introduce the concept, which can be carried forward illustration free ... The power of the theory resides in concepts, not in description' (Glaser 1978: 134). Strauss (1987: 264) makes the point even more directly when he states that 'interview and field-note quotations tend to be brief, and often are woven in with the analysis within the same or closely related sentences.'

Nevertheless, it should be noted that in a study of this kind some sorts of description are impossible in any case. A number of the subjects pursued in the interviews were too superficial for lengthy discussion, a problem that may be endemic to life-style research in general (Glyptis 1989a: 38–47). Moreover, because the leisure lives of Franco-Calgarians, like those of other city dwellers, unfold mostly in the privacy of their families and networks of friends, those lives cannot be systematically observed by outsiders, including researchers. For this reason the use of observations and interviews in the ethnographic study of symbolic communities in large cities appears to be limited. When the research subjects are widely scattered and many of their activities are effectively private, the field sociologist has the subjects' accounts about the latter as his or her only source of information.

8 When dealing with status groups, of which the francophone communities outside Quebec are an example, Veal (1989: 143–4) suggests that we use the Weberian concept of status to theoretically link the concepts of life-style and social structure. Here is a potentially fruitful way of joining the cultural and structural approaches just mentioned.

9 My conception of culture is anthropological and I believe fairly standard. It is a group's collective stock of knowledge, art, ideas, customs, values, norms, beliefs, laws, goals, outlooks, technologies, activities, and patterns of behaviour. With the exception of laws a local urban francophone culture rooted in minority circumstances could consist of all of these.

10 Given the political status of Canadian francophones in their own country it is arguable whether their social-scientific examination is accurately classified as part of ethnic studies. For this same reason, extending research findings in ethnic studies to the study of Franco-Canadians is fraught with difficulties.

11 Kelly (1993) reaches a similar conclusion in a recent exploratory study of different types of workers. He points out that social roles intersect. Thus, life cannot be neatly separated into exclusive domains and similar dimensions of meaning, including leisure, overlap several roles.

Chapter 2

1 The hypothesis that Fort la Jonquière was built in the neighbour-

hood in 1751 and because of that fact was the first francophone establishment in the region is now of doubtful validity (MacEwan 1984: 75–9). Its true location is now believed to be in Saskatchewan.

2 The remainder of this chapter is based substantially on the works of three authors: Rolande Parel (1987), Robert Stamp (1980), and Donald B. Smith (1985).

3 In 1991 the Department of the Secretary of State published a set of 'Summary Reports' on the nature of francophone minority communities in all the provinces except Quebec. The reports show that francophones control French-language education only in New Brunswick and certain counties in Ontario. Elsewhere they are denied this responsibility to a significant degree, notwithstanding its guarantee in Article 23 of the Charter of Rights and Freedoms. This discrepancy is taken up again in chapter 9.

4 The federal government is not the only source of outside funding for projects leading to realization of the four goals, only the most generous. The Bureau of Quebec also grants funds for francophone community projects implemented outside Quebec but somehow related to it. And, depending on the nature of the project, financial support may be obtained in Alberta from provincial or municipal agencies or from provincially run lotteries. At one time the Catholic church gave money for these purposes.

5 This is our working definition of 'French school,' which serves well in this book. Still another, narrower, more political definition is sometimes used in francophone regions outside Quebec when battling the authorities for educational control: a (true) French school is as just defined, but only if it is managed by francophones.

6 These figures were provided by the staff at École Sainte-Anne.

7 The Aquitaine school operated only in the morning, leaving the afternoon open for instruction in English at one of the Calgary schools if the child's parents wanted this.

Chapter 3

1 These findings square with those recently reported by Statistics Canada, to the effect that among couples speaking the same mother tongue, the first language their children learn is nearly

always that of the couple. This holds even when they are living in minority circumstances (Turcotte 1993: 17).

2 Although I lack systematic evidence on the matter, my interviews and conversations suggest that francophones are more likely than anglophones to sing at home and at public gatherings. One possible partial explanation of this tendency comes from an observation made by Tétu de Labsade (1990: 328–9) that historically, Quebecers were much inclined to sing at home on all sorts of occasions.

3 The Copains de Jeux also organize strictly adult events during the school year, including monthly suppers and workshops for parents.

4 French-English bilingualism, however, has increased over this period, a point considered in greater detail in chapter 8.

Chapter 4

1 This preference among francophone and mixed couples for all-French schooling for their children is corroborated by the respondents of this study who taught in the immersion schools. These respondents reported that their pupils came by and large from homogeneous anglophone families. Nonetheless, I encountered the occasional francophone couple who were sending one or more of their children to all-English schools expressly for the purpose of learning English. Usually the couple had moved to Calgary for the same reason.

2 It was rare for an interviewee to criticize the quality of French teaching at the immersion schools. On the contrary, the quality was generally judged to be as good as found in the French schools. The chief worry was with the influence anglophone students have on their francophone peers.

Chapter 5

1 I am indebted to Stanley Parker for calling my attention to this possibility.

2 The French Centre is officially available to all Franco-Calgarians, but its inaccessible location may be one reason why many would-be participants from outside the University fail to frequent it.

3 A Thursday evening equivalent, which attracted somewhat more men, has recently been discontinued because of a lack of interest.

4 The improvisation leagues are popular with French Canadians in many parts of the country, and especially in Quebec. Typically, several teams compete within the framework of a hockey league, where they accumulate points for winning 'matches' and where, at the end of the season, some of them participate in the 'playoffs.' The nearest equivalent in English Canada to the ligues d'improvisation is Keith Johnstone's Theatresports (see Stebbins 1990: 28, 62).

Chapter 6

1 Krysan and D'Antonio (1992: 2231–2) define voluntary organizations as groups independent of control from sources outside themselves, where people are free to join or leave and where members establish their own objectives and goals as well as the means to achieve them.

2 To counteract their professional isolation from everyday French, some translators regularly watch television or read periodicals such as *l'Actualité* expressly to remain abreast of new vocabulary.

3 La tête fromagée or la tête de fromage are French-Canadian equivalents of the French le fromage de tête.

4 Columnist Don Braid (1989) came across such a case in St. Paul, a small city in central Alberta. He described how francophones there consistently vote for the federal Conservative Party and more recently the Reform Party, even though the members of parliament they elect consistently vote against their linguistic interests and sometimes even make insulting public remarks about them. Braid says that 'the explanation, according to thoughtful French speakers in the area, is rooted in subservience. The French have always delegated their authority first to the Church, then to the English-speaking business élite that began to dominate after the Second World War.' The implication is that the francophones living outside Quebec away from the large cities prefer to leave the local leadership to others.

Chapter 7

1 Some time ago when the number of québécois francophones in

Calgary was higher, ACFA organized public réveillons for two consecutive years. To my knowledge, these have not even been attempted since.

2 Franco-Calgarians, however, had a chance to participate in October 1993, in a similar event organized this time by the ACFA under the banner of Gala de la Francophonie.

3 Notwithstanding Calgary's tendency to celebrate La Saint-Jean-Baptiste rather than the Fête Nationale du Québec, this day is being referred to more and more outside Quebec as the Fête Nationale des Canadiens-Français.

4 This idea of cultural bridge is limited to its implication that variations in life-style can be experienced by entering the everyday affairs of another linguistic community. A cultural bridge, as conceived of here, is essentially informal; it is not therefore a political bridge, which leads to formal links with, for example, the power structure of the wider majority community. An example of an analysis of the latter is provided by Breton (1991).

Chapter 8

1 In a small number of families one or both of the parents were fluent in a third language, usually Spanish, which they wanted their children to learn as well.

2 Dubbed versions of a film can be annoying inasmuch as the lips of the actors are not completely synchronized with their words and the dubbed voices may not fit the characters as well as they do in the original.

3 Some francophones worry further that postal workers might not understand some of these words. Still, in the past three years I have carried out three large-scale mailings to Franco-Calgarians using envelopes addressed in precisely this way. I have no evidence whatsoever of any mutilation or misunderstanding.

Chapter 9

1 One favourable sign that the federal government will not forsake its commitment to bilingualism and francophone communities outside Quebec came on 20 May 1993. On that day Monique Landry, the

Secretary of State, announced that she had advanced $112 million over six years for the management of French primary and secondary schools and the development of French postsecondary institutions. Calgary's proposed school-community centre is said to be in line to receive some of this money.

2 Landry and Allard (1990) come to a similar conclusion in the course of explicating their macroscopic model of personal bilingual development.

References

Allaire, Gratien. 1988. Pour la survivance, l'association canadienne-française de l'Alberta. In *Les outils de la francophonie*, edited by Monique Bournot-Trites, William Bruneau, and Robert Roy. Saint-Boniface, Man.: Centre d'Études Franco-Canadiennes de l'Ouest
– 1991. La construction d'une culture française dans l'Ouest canadien, la diversité originelle. Paper presented at the Séminaire de la Chair pour le developpement de la recherche sur la culture d'expression française en Amérique du nord, Winter, at Laval University, Quebec
Almgren, Gunnar. 1992. Community. In *Encyclopedia of sociology*, Vol. 1. edited by Edgar F. Borgatta and Marie L. Borgatta. New York: Macmillan
Anderson, Alan B. 1985a. Ethnic identity in francophone communities in Saskatchewan, Research Report No. 6. Saskatoon, Sask.: University of Saskatchewan, Research Unit for French-Canadian Studies
– 1985b. French settlements in Saskatchewan: Historical and demographic perspectives. Research Report No. 5. Saskatoon, Sask.: University of Saskatchewan, Research Unit for French-Canadian Studies
Association for Canadian Studies. 1989. *Demolinguistic trends and the evolution of Canadian institutions.* Montreal
Beaudoin, Réjean. 1988. Les nouveaux francophones dans un milieu multiculturelle. In *Les outils de la francophonie.* edited by Monique Bournot-Trites, William Bruneau, and Robert Roy. Saint-Boniface, Man.: Winnipeg: Centre d'Études Franco-Canadiennes de l'Ouest

Bélanger, Daniel. 1992. Les francophones de la Colombie-Britannique: une communauté invisible et volatile. *Le Franco*, 20 mars

Bella, Leslie. 1992. *The Christmas imperative: Leisure, family, and women's work*. Halifax: Fernwood Books

Bernard, Roger. 1988. *De québécois à ontarois*. Hearst, Ont.: Le Nordir

– 1991. Éduquer en français au Canada: Conjoncture socio-démographique. *Éducation et francophone* (Les actes du 44e congrès de l'Association Canadienne Française d'Éducation de Langue Française) 19 décembre, special issue: 20–25

Berscheid, Ellen. 1985. Interpersonal Attraction. In *The handbook of social psychology*. 3rd ed. vol. 2, edited by Gardner Lindzey and Elliot Aronson. New York: Random House

Bertrand, Alain. 1992. Parc soleil devient Terres des jeunes. *Le Calgaréen*, juin

– 1993. Société Franco-Canadienne ou ACFA? *Le Franco*, 26 février.

Bishop, Jeff, and Paul Hoggett. 1986. *Organizing around enthusiams: Mutual aid in leisure*. London: Comedia Publishing Group

Bocquel, Bernard. 1990. Le français et les minorités francophones dans l'Ouest canadien. *Cahiers franco-canadiens de l'Ouest* 2: 113–21

Braid, Don. 1989. French-Albertans must think Tories speak their language. *Calgary Herald*, 18 March, sec. A3

Breton, Raymond. 1964. Institutional completeness of ethnic communities and the personal relations of immigrants. *American Journal of Sociology* 70: 193–205

– 1991. *The Governance of ethnic communities: Political structures and processes in Canada*. New York: Greenwood

Breton, Raymond, Wsevolod W. Isajiw, Warren E. Kalbach, and Jeffrey G. Reitz. 1990. *Ethnic identity and equality*. Toronto: University of Toronto Press

Brightbill, Charles K. 1961. *Man and leisure: A philosophy of recreation*. Englewood Cliffs, N.J.: Prentice-Hall

Bryan, Hobson. 1977. Leisure value systems and recreational specialization: The case of trout fishermen. *Journal of Leisure Research* 9:174–87

Caillé, Mélanie. 1993. De l'argent pour le centre scolaire communautaire. *Le Franco*, 13 août

Cardinal, Linda, and Jean Lapointe. 1989. La sociologie des francophones hors Québec. Paper presented at the Annual Meetings of the Canadian Ethnic Studies Association, Calgary

Le Chaînon (Edmonton). 1992. Inscriptions dans les écoles francophones de l'Alberta. 6 (septembre)

– 1993. Tous les marriages mixtes ne produisent pas les mêmes résultats. 7 (avril)

Chambré, Susan M. 1987. Good deads in old age: Volunteering by the new leisure class. Lexington, Mass.: Lexington Books

Churchill, Stacey, and Isabel Kaprielian-Churchill. 1991. The Future of francophone and Acadian communities in a pluralistic society: Facing pluralism. Ottawa: Fédération des Communautés Francophones et Acadiennes du Canada

Cohen, Anthony P. 1985. The symbolic construction of community. London: Tavistock

Commissioner of Official Languages. 1988. Language policy. In The Canadian encyclopedia 2d ed. vol. 2. Edmonton, Alta.: Hurtig

– 1989. Annual Report 1989. Ottawa: Ministry of Supply and Services, Government of Canada

Cosman, Carl. 1993. Let's talk: English-French bilingualism in Canada. Language and Society, no. 44 (Fall): 14–15

Couture, Claude. 1992. Tradition, modernité et Canada français. In Après dix ans ... bilan et prospective, edited by Gratien Allaire, Paul Dubé, and Gamila Morcos. Edmonton: Institute de Recherche de la Faculté Saint-Jean, Université de l'Alberta

Couturier, Bertin. 1991. Mobilisation autour des centres scolaires communautaires. Le Franco, 31 mai

Dawson, C. 1991. English only at Coffee Break. Calgary Herald, 18 October

Dawson, C.A. 1936. Group settlements: Ethnic communities in Western Canada. Toronto: Macmillan

Dupont, Jean-Claude, and Jacques Mathieu, eds. 1986. Héritage de la francophonie canadienne, traditions orales. Sainte-Foy, Québec: Les Presses de l'Université Laval

Fine, Gary A. 1988. Dying for a laugh. Western Folklore 47: 177–94

Fischer, Lucy R., and Kay B. Schaffer. 1993. Older volunteers: A guide to research and practice. Newbury Park, Calif.: Sage

Le Franco. 1993. 23 avril

Glaser, Barney G. 1978. *Theoretical sensitivity.* Mill Valley, Calif.: The Sociology Press

Glaser, Barney G., and Anselm L. Strauss. 1967. *The discovery of grounded theory.* Chicago: Aldine

Glyptis, Sue. 1989a. Lifestyles and leisure patterns – methodological approaches. In *Life styles: Theories, concepts, methods, and results of life style research in international perspective,* edited by Blanka Filipcova, Sue Glyptis, and Walter Tokarski. Prague, Czechoslovakia: Academy of Sciences

– 1989b. *Leisure and unemployment.* Milton Keynes, Eng.: Open University Press

Godbout, L. 1992. L'Identité prétendue et l'identité vécue d'après le discours de Franco-Albertains. In *Après dix ans: bilan et prospective,* edited by Gratien Allaire, Paul Dubé, and Gamila Morcos. Edmonton: Institut de Recherche de la Faculté Saint-Jean, Université de l'Alberta

Gold, Gerald L. 1975. *St. Pascal.* Toronto: Holt, Rinehart & Winston

Goldenberg, Sheldon, and Valerie A. Haines. 1992. Social networks and institutional completeness: From territory to ties. *Canadian Journal of Sociology* 17: 301

Gordon, C. Wayne, and Nicholas Babchuk. 1959. A Typology of voluntary associations. *American Sociological Review* 24: 22–9

Grabb, Edward G., and James E. Curtis. 1992. Voluntary association activity in English Canada, French Canada, and the United States. *Canadian Journal of Sociology* 17: 371–88

Grenier, G. 1990. Bilingualism among anglophones and francophones in Canada. In *Demolinguistic trends and the evolution of Canadian institutions.* Montreal: Association for Canadian Studies

Hastings, Donald W., Donald A. Clelland, and Robin L. Danielson. 1982. Gordon's assimilation paradigm: The issues of ethnic communality, insularity, and return migration. In *Research in race and ethnic relations.* vol. 3, edited by Rutledge Dennis. Greenwich, Conn.: JAI

Hastings, Donald W., Suzanne Kurth, and Judith Meyer. 1989. Competitive swimming careers through the life course. *Sociology of Sport Journal* 6: 278–84

Hébert, Yvonne. 1993. MOI, mes AMIS, mon École: l'adolescent en milieu minoritaire. Paper presented at the Colloque sur la recherche en milieu minoritaire, annual congress of the Association Canadienne Française pour l'Avancement des Sciences, mai, Rimouski, Québec

Hébert, Yvonne, and Robert A. Stebbins. 1993. La francophonie de Calgary: Une étude démolinguistique. In *Une langue qui pense: la recherche en milieu minoritaire francophone au Canada*, edited by Linda Cardinal. Ottawa: Les Presses de l'Université d'Ottawa

Heller, Monica, and Laurette Lévy. 1992. Mixed marriages: Life on the linguistic frontier. *Multilingua* 11: 11–43

Henderson, Karla. 1981. Motivation and perception of volunteerism as a leisure activity. *Journal of Leisure Research* 13: 208–18

Hillary, George A., Jr. 1955. Definitions of community: Areas of agreement. *Rural Sociology* 20: 111–23

Irvine, William P. 1990. Segmented language communities and bilingualism: Towards segmented language use? In *Demolinguistic trends and the evolution of Canadian institutions*. Montreal: Association for Canadian Studies

Jackson, John D. 1988. *Community and conflict: A study of French-English relations in Ontario*. Rev. ed. Toronto: Canadian Scholars Press

Jones, Richard. 1988. St-Jean-Baptiste Society. In *The Canadian encyclopedia*. Vol. 3. 2nd ed. Edmonton: Hurtig

Joy, Richard J. 1992. *Canada's official languages: The progess of bilingualism*. Toronto: University of Toronto Press

Kaplan, Max. 1975. *Leisure: Theory and policy*. New York: Wiley

Kellert, Stephen R. 1985. Birdwatching in American society. *Leisure Sciences* 7: 343–60

Kelly, John R. 1990. *Leisure*. 2nd ed. Englewood Cliffs, N.J.: Prentice-Hall

– 1993. Multiple dimensions of meaning in the domains of work, family, and leisure. Paper presented at the Centenary Congress of the International Institute of Sociology, June, Paris, France

Krysan, Maria, and William D'Antonio. 1992. Voluntary associations. In *Encyclopedia of sociology*. Vol. 4, edited by Edgar F. Borgatta and Marie L. Borgatta. New York: Macmillan

Lambert, Wallace E. 1975. Culture and language as factors in learning and education. In *Education of immigrant students*, edited by Aaron Wolfgang. Toronto: Ontario Institute for Studies in Education

Landry, Rodrigue, and Réal Allard. 1990. Contact des langues and développement bilingue: un modèle macroscopique. *La revue canadienne des langues vivantes* 46: 527–53

Leroux, Carole, and Louise Dubé. 1993. La francophonie à Calgary. Rapport du projet d'évaluation et d'orientation présenté à l'Association Canadienne-Française de l'Alberta, régionale de Calgary, mai, Calgary, Alberta

Le Tourneau, Léo. 1988. La francophonie de l'ouest: après l'école, quoi? In *Les outils de la francophonie*, edited by Monique Bournot-Trites, William Bruneau, and Robert Roy. Saint-Boniface, Man.: Centre d'Études franco-canadiennes de l'ouest

MacEwan, Grant. 1984. *French in the West/Les franco-canadians dans l'ouest*. Saint-Boniface, Man.: Éditions des plaines

Maxwell, Thomas R. 1971. La population d'origine française de l'agglomération métropolitaine de Toronto. *Recherches sociographiques* 12: 319–44

Orthner, Dennis K. 1975. Leisure activity patterns and marital satisfaction over the marital career. *Journal of Marriage and the Family* 37: 91–104

Parel, Rolande. 1987. The French roots. In *Citymakers: Calgarians after the frontier.* edited by Max Foran and Shellagh Jameson. Calgary: The Historical Society of Alberta, Chinook Country Chapter

Pitre, Martin. 1992. Une innovation acadienne dans la quincaillerie des outils de développement. *Le devoir*, 13 juin, Cahier spécial/'Francophonie canadienne.'

Poulin, Jeanne. 1992. Quebec Culture: Folkoric or International? *The New Federation*, 3 (July/August): 22–4

Rayside, David M. 1991. *A small town in modern times: Alexandria, Ontario.* Montreal and Kingston: McGill–Queen's University Press

Ross, David P. 1990. Economic dimension of volunteer work in Canada. Ottawa: Report prepared for the Department of the Secretary of State, January

Savas, Daniel. 1991. Insitutions francophones et vitalité communautaire: motivations symboliques et fonctionnelles du choix de réseau institutionnel. In *À la mesure du pays* ... , edited by Jean-Guy

Quenneville. Saint-Boniface, Man.: Centre d'Études Franco-Canadiennes de l'Ouest

Shaffir, William B., and Robert A. Stebbins (eds.). 1991. *Experiencing
fieldwork: An inside view of qualitative research in the social sciences.*
Newbury Park, Calif.: Sage.

Shaw, Susan M. 1985. The meaning of leisure in everyday life. *Leisure
Sciences* 7: 1–24

Smith, Donald B. 1985. A history of French-speaking Albertans. In
Peoples of Alberta, edited by Harold Palmer and Tamara Palmer.
Saskatoon, Sask.: Western Producer Prairie Books

Sobel, Michael E. 1981. *Lifestyle and social structure: Concepts, definitions,
analyses.* New York: Academic Press

Société Radio-Canada. 1992. *Les beaux dimanches.* 29 décembre

Stamp, Robert. 1980. French and Catholic. *Calgary Magazine* 2 (9):
68–70, 86–89

Statistics Canada. 1980. *An overview of volunteer workers in Canada*, DBS
Catalogue 71–530. Ottawa: Supply and Services Canada

Statistics Canada. Census Division. 1984. *Highlights: 1981 census of
Canada.* DBS Catalogue 92–X–535E. Ottawa: Supply and Services
Canada

– 1992. *Mother tongue – 1991 Census Technical Reports*, DBS Catalogue
93–313. Ottawa: Supply and Services Canada

– 1993. *Home language and mother tongue – the Nation–Census of Canada*,
1991, DBS Catalogue 93–317. Ottawa: Supply and Services Canada

Stebbins, Robert A. 1981a. Toward a social psychology of stage fright.
In *Sport in the sociocultural process*, edited by Marie Hart and Susan
Birrell. Dubuque, Iowa: W.C. Brown

– 1990. *The laugh-makers: Stand-up comedy as art, business, and life-style.*
Montreal and Kingston: McGill-Queen's University Press

– 1992a. Concatenated exploration: Notes on a neglected type of
longitudinal research. *Quality & Quantity* 26: 435–42

– 1992b. *Amateurs, professionals and serious leisure.* Montreal and
Kingston: McGill-Queen's University Press

– 1992c. Famille, bilinguisme et style de vie francophone en milieu
minoritaire. Paper presented at the Colloque sur l'État et Les
Minorités, November, Saint-Boniface, Manitoba

– 1993a. Becoming a barbershop singer. In *Barbershopping: Musical and social harmony*, edited by Max Kaplan. Cranbury, NJ: Associated Universities

- 1993b. Le style de vie francophone en milieu minoritaire. *Cahiers franco-canadiens de l'Ouest* 5: 177–93
- In press. The liberal arts hobbies: A neglected subtype of serious leisure. *Loisir et société*

Strauss, Anselm L. 1987. *Qualitative analysis for social scientists.* New York: Cambridge University Press.

Taylor, John. 1988. Ottawa. In *The Canadian encyclopedia*, Vol. 3. 2nd ed. Edmonton: Hurtig

Tellier, Sylvain. 1993. British Columbia's francophones. *Language and Society* 44 (Fall): 6–8

Tétu de Labsade, Françoise. 1990. *Le Québec: un pays une culture.* Montreal: Boréal/Seuil

Thériault, J.-Yvon. 1990. The future of the French-speaking community outside Quebec: A tug of war. In *Demolinguistic trends and the evolution of Canadian institutions.* Montreal: Association for Canadian Studies

Turcotte, Pierre. 1993. Mixed language couples and their children. *Canadian Social Trends*, 29 (Summer): 15–17

Unruh, David R. 1980. The nature of social worlds. *Pacific Sociological Review* 23: 271–96

Valade, André. 1993. Beaucoup de visiteurs, peu d'exposants. *Le Franco*, 14 mai

Vallee, Frank G. 1971. Regionalism and Ethnicity: The French-Canadian case. In *Minority Canadians*, vol. 2, edited by Jean L. Elliott. Scarborough, Ont.: Prentice-Hall of Canada

Van Maanen, John. 1988. *Tales of the field: On writing ethnography.* Chicago: University of Chicago Press

Van Til, Jon. 1988. *Mapping the third sector: Voluntarism in a changing political economy.* New York: The Foundation Center

Veal, A.J. 1989. Leisure, lifestyle and status: A pluralist framework for analysis. *Leisure Studies* 8: 141–53

- 1993. The concept of lifestyle: A review. *Leisure Studies* 12: 233–52

Villeneuve, Paul-Y. 1983. Maillardville: à l'ouest rien de nouveau. In *Du continent perdu à l'archipel retrouvé: le Québec et L'Amérique française*, edited by Dean R. Louder and Eric Waddell. Québec: Les Presses de l'Université Laval

Yair, Gad. 1990. The commitment to long-distance running and level of activities. *Journal of Leisure Research* 22: 213–27

Zurcher, Louis A., Jr., R. George Kirkpatrick, Robert G. Cushing, and Charles K. Bowman. 1971. The anti-pornography campaign: A symbolic crusade. *Social Problems* 19: 217–38

Index